Endorsements
Fast Track to Masterful Coaching

One Challenge affirms the centrality of coaching in the lifelong development of our members and in the growth of healthy teams. I'm thrilled that the Lord has brought Dr. Walt Hastings—as a Master Certified Coach—to equip OC's people and deepen our culture of Spirit-led coaching. The concepts in this book are power tools for people with a Barnabas spirit. Put them to work and watch God transform lives, communities, and nations!
—Dean Carlson, president, One Challenge

No matter your ministry focus, coaching can be a powerful method by which you can serve, sharpen, and grow others. OC is blessed to have Dr. Walt Hastings as one of us—an OC member with a wealth of training and experience, coupled with a heart to serve in and through our agency. You will find his book a valuable resource and guide as you seek to enhance the effectiveness of your ministry—and for your personal growth as well. I commend Walt and his book to you!
—David Bulger, vice president,
One Challenge Global Ministries

If you aspire to quickly grasp the fundamentals of Christian coaching and pursue certification through the International Coach Federation, I highly recommend Fast Track to Masterful Coaching *by Walt Hastings. His explanation of how coaching is*

distinct from other people-helping approaches found in chapter 1 is one of the best you will find in print today. Well done, Walt!
—Gary B. Reinecke, MCC, DMin, executive director,
InFocus Ministries

Fast Track to Masterful Coaching *is a rich primer on coaching, giving a thorough introduction to new coaches, as well as providing a road map toward deeper coaching for experienced coaches. Walt's CHRISP model is a compass that orients coaches to the structure of a powerful coaching conversation, while always keeping the true potential front and center. Well done, Walt!*
—Barbara Richards, MCC, Coach University faculty

Walt shares a deep understanding of the core coaching competencies for anyone wanting to acquire coaching skills. He has developed a new model that gives coaches a roadmap to guide them in engaging in effective coaching conversations. This is a book that will find a home on any coach's short list of handy references.
—Jan Marie Dore, MCC, CPA, Coach University
faculty, Certified Master Business Coach

Coaching is a way of helping others move forward, and Walt Hastings is a masterful coach. While there are no short-cuts to becoming a great coach, in this book Walt shares the essentials that will provide faster growth toward mastery.
—Chad Hall, MCC, DMin, president, Coach
Approach Ministries

Fast Track to Masterful Coaching *is an excellent resource for coaches who want a simple and direct way to approach their faith-based coaching with a clear and easy to remember model.*

God gives us our gifts, our gift to God is how we share those gifts. Walt's CHRISP coaching model simplifies the delivery of those gifts for all coaches. A great addition to any library!
    —Shawna Corden, MCC, Coach University faculty, author
    of *Coach Culture*

Fast Track to Masterful Coaching *is a comprehensive guide that clearly outlines and explores the core competencies, the CHRISP coaching model and many resources, tools and concepts that will prove beneficial to any coach who is interested in building a joyful and fulfilling practice.*
    —Jamee Tenzer, MCC, BCC

In Fast Track to Masterful Coaching *Dr. Walt Hastings delivers exactly what he promises. This is a clear and comprehensive guide to the most important perspectives and skills needed by anyone who wishes to become a competent and, eventually, a masterful coach. His presentation of the Core Competencies of the ICF will be extremely useful to someone working toward credentialing by that organization, as well as to anyone who is considering the credentials of a coach they might engage. Congratulations to Dr. Hastings for creating such a useful resource.*
    —Laurie Weiss, Ph.D., MCC, author,
    Letting It Go: Relieve Anxiety and Toxic

Fast Track
to
Masterful
Coaching

Unlocking the Secret *with the* CHRISP Model

Walt Hastings, MCC

ILLUMIFY
MEDIA.COM

Fast Track to Masterful Coaching

Copyright © 2024 by Walt Hastings

Published by

Illumify Media Global

www.IllumifyMedia.com

"Let's bring your book to life!"

Paperback ISBN: 978-1-949021-92-9

Cover design by Debbie Lewis

Printed in the United States of America

Contents

Section IV:
Former ICF Core Competencies and Other Coaching Skills

Section V: Growing in Your Coaching Skills

Introduction

THIS BOOK IS PRESENTED as a training tool for those persons interested in acquiring coaching skills as quickly as possible. The materials were developed initially as a resource for training field workers and leaders with One Challenge International. One Challenge (often shortened to OC International) is a mission organization that has embraced coaching as a way to train and develop leaders. The CHRISP model presented herein acknowledges our Christian perspective and worldview. The term "CHRISP" is an acronym employed as a memory device. It stands for **C**onnect, **H**omework, **R**esult Desired, **I**nvestigate, **S**teps, **P**urpose. Persons who do not embrace Christianity, but desire to pursue excellent coaching skills undoubtedly will find the book to be useful.

SECTION I

An Introduction to Coaching

1

What Is Coaching?

WHAT IS COACHING?

WHAT IS COACHING? THE etymology of the word *coach* originated before automobiles, airplanes and trains had been invented. Back then a coach was something you rode in, a carriage pulled by horses that got you from where you were to where you wanted to be. Cars today still often carry the label "coach" to describe their types. Thus, a coach is someone who takes you from where you are now to where you want to be.

Coaching, in a nutshell, asks three basic questions.

- Where are you now?
- Where do you want to be?
- How will you get there?

DEFINITIONS OF COACHING

Coaching has been defined in various ways. The International Coaching Federation (ICF) is the largest organization that seeks to provide oversight and direction to the coaching profession. It defines coaching as "partnering with clients in a thought-provoking and creative process that inspires them to maximize their personal and professional potential."[1]

Val Hastings, founder of the coaching school Coaching4TodaysLeaders offers the following definition:

"Coaching is a partnership that accelerates what is already underway or about to begin, that maximizes potential, moving people from good to great."[2]

Keith Webb, who founded the coaching school Creative Results Management (CRM), brings a spiritual perspective: "Coaching is an ongoing intentional conversation that empowers a person or group to fully live out God's calling."[3]

These three definitions help provide an understanding about coaching. Coaching is a non-directive intentional conversation in which a person partners with another to help them gain clarity or new perspectives. Ideally, the person successfully moves toward their goals while achieving personal and professional growth.

KEY COMPONENTS OF COACHING

A skillful coach keeps these key things in mind.

- Coaching is a partnership.
- Coaching is a mindset.
- Coaching is a process.
- Coaching is client centered.
- Coaching produces a shift.

A Partnership. The coach comes alongside as a partner rather than from a position of authority or as an expert. While the partnership is one of equality, the focus is not equal, in that the attention is always on the client rather than on the coach. It is a relationship of trust. Safety and trust are essential for the partnership to succeed.

A Mindset. The coach comes to the relationship not to "fix" the person, but sees the person as already whole and complete.

Rather than having a fix-it mentality, the coach looks for the person's strengths, gifts, and greatness. One university professor begins each course by informing the students that they all have an A. The coach approaches each new relationship giving the person an A.

Client Centered. Coaching is all about the person being coached, not about the coach. Coaching shines the spotlight on the client, not the coach. A fact that highlights this reality is that the client always has responsibility to bring the topic or issue upon which to focus.

A Process. Sometimes a single conversation can help resolve a problem or issue. However, coaching usually is a process with ongoing conversations producing powerful results. The coach empowers clients through self-discovery. They gain clarity and awareness as the coach asks powerful questions, listens deeply, and occasionally offers feedback or shares observations. While the client brings the content, the coach gives direction to the process, guiding conversations to be most productive for the client.

A Shift. When speeding toward one's destination in an automobile, the car shifts from a lower gear into a higher one the faster you go. In coaching, shifts also occur in a person's perspective, providing clarity or understanding. The person suddenly sees things from a completely new point of view. Such shifts are desirable and celebrated by the coach since they allow the client to move more quickly toward goals.

HOW COACHING DIFFERS FROM OTHER WAYS OF HELPING

Coaching is a well-defined way of helping others. It has similarities and differences from mentoring, consulting, counseling, and therapy. All of these approaches are worthwhile and are to be embraced as important ways of helping. However, coaching is to be viewed as a separate approach, not to be confused with these other methodologies.

Mentoring. When some hear the word *coach*, they think mentor. Both coaching and mentoring are valid ways of helping others learn and grow, but they are at opposite ends of the helping continuum. Stated in the extreme, mentoring is a directive or telling approach, while coaching is a non-directive or listening approach.

A mentor often comes to a relationship as the authority or the expert, assuming a role of predominance based upon greater knowledge, skills, and experience. At times, the client is so new in a certain area that they lack basic knowledge and experience, so a mentor is needed to help them become knowledgeable and informed. In contrast, the coach comes alongside as a helper, not assuming an authoritative position.

The coach realizes that the one true expert concerning the client is the client him or herself. Therefore, the coach assumes the role of learner, eager to let the "expert," the client, inform the coach of the issues and concerns. The mentor tells the person what they should know or do based upon their superior knowledge and experience. Conversely, the coach uses the skills of asking, listening, and reflecting to help the client bring to light the issues to be addressed.

Sports Coach. It is interesting that the coaching profession (generally acknowledged to have arisen around the mid-1990s) used the same word *coach* to describe its practitioners as do those who provide direction in the sports world. Admittedly, they both have some things in common, such as encouraging, celebrating successes, and acknowledging improvement. But for the most part, sports coaches use a mentoring, or telling, approach in working to improve athletic performance. Using the same word that describes two opposite behavior styles is very confusing to those new to the definition being presented here. (Let the reader beware that when you hear of a sports coach, such as in baseball or football or basketball, you should think mentor and not confuse it with the concept described in these pages.)

Consulting. A consultant typically arrives as an outside expert to help identify, diagnose, and recommend remedies for whatever is not going well. Initially, most consultants will do a good deal of listening, but once a problem is identified, it is their responsibility to recommend solutions. By way of contrast, the coach endeavors to assist the client in identifying the problem as well as drawing out the solutions from the client by asking good questions. In using this approach, the client *owns* the solution and therefore is much more likely to move forward in taking the necessary steps toward resolution. As long as the consultant owns the solution, it is uncertain whether the client will move forward with the recommended steps.

Counseling and Therapy. The tools the coach and the counselor use are similar. Both are fully present, ask good questions, listen well, and occasionally reflect back to the client. The difference is in the perspective each brings. The goal of the counselor or therapist often is to bring healing and wholeness, while the coach already views the client as whole and complete. Generally, the counselor stands in the present with the client and looks to the past, seeking to uncover hurtful experiences. Once these events are brought to light, the counselor strives to help the client gain a new perspective that changes behavior and brings one into a healthy present. On the other hand, the coach stands in the present with the client, looking to the future, seeking to unlock the keys for success for the client's future. Therapy is more about recovery, while coaching is more about discovery.

Another helpful analogy is that of archaeology versus architecture. Therapy is like archaeology in that it digs into the past, hoping to shed light and uncover hidden meanings that will be helpful in the present. Coaching is like architecture in that it builds on the solid present, desiring to design and create a bright future.[4]

Keep in mind the difference between therapy and therapeutic. Coaching is not therapy, and coaches must be able to identify the signs that a referral to a competent therapist is needed. Meanwhile, coaching is therapeutic in that working with a coach and moving toward one's goals makes one feel good and be more positive about oneself.

WHY COACHING?

Why coaching, instead of another approach to helping? Basically, it is because coaching works.

- Coaching creates ownership.
- Coaching involves accountability.
- Coaching generates thinking.
- Coaching moves people forward.
- Coaching supports emerging leaders as they develop.

Coaching Creates Ownership
Because coaching is client centered and non-directive, clients identify their own problems, diagnose their own issues, create their own solutions, and determine the next steps to take. Simply put, coaching creates ownership of solutions rather than solutions being imposed by someone else. When people own their problems and solutions, they are much more likely to carry them out compared to when a solution is imposed on them from the outside.

Coaching Involves Accountability
Knowing that their coach will ask them how a certain action step went motivates clients to move forward and complete their agreed upon activities. Coaching produces ownership and accountability—the two big factors that encourages follow-through.

Coaching Generates Thinking
Coaches ask questions that cause clients to think. Often people think about things they have never thought about before. As they reflect, they see things in a new light. They come to new insights and new perspectives.

Coaching Produces Forward Movement
Coaches encourage people to clarify what is important, dream big, set goals, determine next steps, and take actions to reach those goals. Achieving goals gives people a sense of moving forward, of making progress. Bob Logan, founder of the coaching school CoachNet, observes that clients move about three times faster toward their goals, compared to those who are not being coached.[5]

Coaching Supports Emerging Leaders
When people have to wrestle through their own issues, they are forced to think and to analyze. When people think about what's coming and describe a preferred future, they dream and clarify their own vision. When people strategize and determine next steps, they become more effective planners. When people face the consequences of their actions, they become more responsible. These are the byproducts of using a coaching approach and are some of the ingredients that make for a strong leader. Coaching provides support and encouragement to emerging leaders.

SUMMARY

Coaching is a way of helping others that has emerged only in the last three decades. Simply put, coaching is a way to help people get from where they are to where they want to be. Coaching is a non-directive, intentional conversation whereby a coach partners with someone to help move them toward their goals. Coaching is a client-centered process. It embraces a mindset that seeks to produce a shift in perspectives and behaviors. Coaches applaud other ways of helping, such as mentoring or therapy, and know that a coaching approach works because it creates ownership, accountability, thinking and forward movement. In the process, coaching encourages and supports leaders. Coaching is a wonderful way to partner with people to inspire them to reach their goals and become stronger people.

SECTION II

The CHRISP Coaching Model

2

Overview of the CHRISP Coaching Model

WHY MODELS?

A MODEL IS A representation of something real, an aspect of reality. A model airplane represents a real airplane. A map of Chicago represents the city, its streets and features. A model helps you better understand and navigate the real thing.

While a model is real in that you can see it and touch it, in many cases a model is a miniature form of something much larger. When an architect makes a model of a building yet to be built, for example, that model helps give a perspective on what the bigger object eventually will be. A model can create an image of what you're shooting for.

This is precisely how a coaching model works. A coaching model represents some real truth that is not quite the genuine thing. It is but a representation of what a real coaching conversation might look like. Using a coaching model to get one started in coaching is a bit like using training wheels when a child is learning to ride a bike. It's helpful in the early going, but after a while the training wheels are no longer needed. In fact, they may get in the way of a skilled rider. Likewise, a coaching model helps a coach in the early stages and so is useful and needed.

An effective model portrays some aspect of reality so well that it conveys greater understanding. However, even the best models neglect to describe *everything* about reality. Coaches must not be so focused on a model that they miss the truth about the client with whom they are coaching. After years of coaching, perhaps most coaches find that they rely on their coaching skills to guide them through a coaching conversation rather than depending on a certain model.

MODELS SERVE AS ROADMAPS

Recently I went on a six-thousand-mile road trip. I went to places and cities where I had never been before. I used a road atlas as well as a GPS phone app. Using these aids, I seldom got lost. I found them very useful tools for navigating my way around unfamiliar places.

A coaching roadmap is simply a tool to help new coaches navigate their way around having intentional conversations where they have never been before. A coaching model is a roadmap that keeps them from getting lost in unfamiliar territory. In a sense, a coaching model is a support structure new coaches can use to kickstart their coaching and to keep them on track.

COACHING ROADMAPS HAVE
A NATURAL FLOW

The best coaching roadmaps have a certain natural flow. This natural flow includes these factors that are drawn from the International Coaching Federation's core competencies:

1. Building the relationship
2. Determining what the client wants to accomplish

3. Exploring the issue presented by the client
4. Checking on progress
5. Determining steps the client will take to move forward
6. Affirming value gained from the coaching conversation

There is no lack of coaching roadmaps! Just as one could log onto the internet and choose from a variety of roadmaps that all depict similar cities, states, and areas, so there are a variety of coaching roadmaps from which to choose. Here are some widely used coaching models. A casual reading reveals a natural flow that most models incorporate.

The CLEAR Model (Peter Hawkins)[6]
- C (clear)
- L (listening)
- E (exploring)
- A (action)
- R (review)

The GROW Model (Sir John Whitmore)[7]
- G (goal)
- R (reality)
- O (options)
- W (will)

The Five Rs Model (Bob Logan)[8]
- R (relate)
- R (reflect)
- R (refocus)
- R (resource)
- R (review)

The C.O.A.C.H. Model (Coach University)[9]
- C (celebrate & contract)
- O (observe, obstacles & opportunities)
- A (acknowledge & affirm)
- C (check-in)
- H (hold accountable)

The COACH Model (Keith Webb)[10]
- C (connect)
- O (outcome)
- A (awareness)
- C (course)
- H (highlights)

How do you choose an effective coaching model? It may depend on what coaching school you select since many schools have developed their own model. My earliest coach training was with CoachNet, where I learned and used the Five Rs model. My next training was with Creative Results Management (CRM), where I learned the COACH model and used this model for many years. Then I took advanced coach training with Coach U, where I was introduced to a variety of coaching models. All three schools are recognized by the ICF (International Coaching Federation).

QUESTIONS TO CONSIDER WHEN CHOOSING A MODEL

- Is it simple to remember?
- Is it comprehensive, covering all aspects?
- How well does it line up with the ICF core competencies? (The competencies are explained later.)

- Is it logical in how it progresses through a coaching conversation?
- Does it help build trust in the coaching relationship?
- Does it encourage deep client exploration?
- Does it include creating actions steps to move the client forward?
- Does it encourage deep listening, asking powerful questions, and providing appropriate feedback?
- Is it truly coaching (i.e., non-directive)?

THE CHRISP COACHING MODEL

The CHRISP coaching model is a comprehensive one in which all the above questions can be answered in the affirmative.

Granted, I have invented a new word by putting an *h* in crisp. Let it be a reminder that a coach's communication must be crisp and clean! (Actually, the Urban Dictionary does give this definition: "A man unlike any other. Only the coolest people ever go by the name Chrisp. He is the most awesome, funny, intelligent and extremely handsome man you will ever meet. Can also be used as an adjective.")[11]

The CHRISP Coaching Model

C – H – R – I – S – P

Connect Homework Result Investigate Steps Purpose

A SUMMARY OF THE CHRISP MODEL FOR A COACHING CONVERSATION

Connect
- *Objective*: Build trust and rapport.
- *Key question*: What's been going on in your life since we last talked?
- Other questions:
  o How are you? How have you been?
  o What significant things have happened in your life recently?
  o What insights have come to you since our last conversation?

Homework
- *Objective*: Obtain a progress update on action steps.
- *Key question*: How have you made progress on your action steps?
- Other questions:
  o What forward movement has been made toward your goals?
  o What might you learn (if not completed) from not having completed this action step?
  o How could this action step be broken down into more manageable parts?

Result
- *Objective*: Determine the conversation goal.
- *Key question*: What result do you want to take away from our conversation today?
- Other questions:
  o What's most important for us to work on today?

o What do you want to accomplish by talking about that?

o How can we know that we've accomplished that by the end of our conversation?

o What makes that the most important thing to talk about today?

o What key points must we talk about to cover this issue well?

Investigate

- *Objective*: Explore the current issue.
- *Key question*: What key issues are there in this situation?
- Other questions:
  o What other factors are influencing this situation?
  o What's another perspective from which we could look at this issue?

Steps

- *Objective*: Capture insights into two or three actionable steps.
- *Key question*: What steps could you to take to move forward?
- Other questions:
  o How can we word this action so that it is SMART (Specific, Measurable, Achievable, Relevant, Timebound)
  o What support do you need?
  o What resources are needed to accomplish this step? Where can you obtain those resources?
  o How committed are you to completing this action by our next coaching conversation?
  o What obstacles might prevent you from completing this action step?

o   What accountability structures would be helpful?

Purpose
- *Objective*: Review and highlight learning.
- *Key question*: How well did we accomplish our purpose in this conversation?
- Other questions:
  o   What value have you gotten from our conversation?
  o   What are your takeaways from today's session?
  o   What do you want to remember from today's session?
  o   What new insights do you have as a result of our talk?
  o   What was most useful to you from our conversation?

CONCLUSION

The CHRISP model is a comprehensive guide to a coaching conversation. Numerous fine road maps have been created for coaches. However, all of them leave out at least one essential element not clearly stated in the outline. I have developed the CHRISP model because it touches all the bases required to have a complete and thorough coaching conversation with a logical flow.

3

Phase 1: C = Connect

THE FIRST PHASE IN the CHRISP coaching model is *connect*. Connect relates closely to the ICF Core Competency 4, Cultivates Trust and Safety.[12] What does it mean to connect? The word *connect* comes from two words in Latin: *con* and *nectere*. *Con* means "with"; *nectere* means "to tie." To connect means "to join, to unite, or to fasten together."[13] To connect is more than just being present together. You are with someone and bound together in a relationship.

For a coach to connect with a client means that you know each other, that you get along together, and that you understand and appreciate each other. You have a relationship and are joined together. There is a link between the two of you. You are united with a bond. What is the bond or glue that holds you together? It is mutual respect, rapport, and trust.

IMPORTANCE OF TRUST

What is trust? It is knowing that you are concerned about my welfare. It is believing that you have my best interests in mind. It is the confidence that you would never knowingly hurt or demean me.

How is trust developed? Trust takes time. It develops slowly, little by little. Trust is aided by self-disclosure, so that I know and understand more and more about you. It is strengthened by consistency, behaving the same, so I know what to expect from you.

Trust is the key to experiencing a deep connection with a client. It has been my observation that it typically takes four or five sessions with clients before they begin to trust me deeply enough to really open up and share sensitive issues with me.

COACHING CREDIBILITY – TRUST REQUIRED

What would make someone want to seek you out to be their coach? Several reasons can be considered, including positional credibility, expertise credibility, spiritual credibility, and relational credibility.

- Perhaps someone would want you to be their coach because of a position you hold, such as a pastor or leader of an organization. That would be *positional* credibility.
- Someone may want you to be their coach because you are a recognized expert in your field, or you are very knowledgeable about a certain subject. That would be *expertise* credibility.
- Possibly someone would want you to be their coach because they regard you as spiritually mature and close to God. That would be *spiritual* credibility.
- As important as each of these kinds of credibility are, the reason that someone would want to continue having you as their coach is because of *relational* credibility. You have proven yourself trustworthy. They know that they can count on you. In a word, they trust you. Trust is foundational for all successful coaching relationships.

THE FIVE LEVELS OF COMMUNICATION

How can you determine the level of trust between you and a client? You can observe at what level they are sharing emotionally.

In healthy relationships where deep levels of trust exist, people feel safe and are willing to take risks by letting others know them deeply. The depth of trust in a relationship can be determined by observing the levels of intimacy at which people share. John Powell popularized the five levels of intimacy in his book *Why Am I Afraid to Tell You Who I Am?* At each level of communication people reveal more of themselves, so the risk factor rises.

1. Level **one** communication is the *sharing of superficialities* (such as the weather or clichés) that serve to simply acknowledge others.
2. Level **two** communication is the *sharing of facts and information* that serves as a way to establish contact.
3. Level **three** communication is *sharing ideas and opinions.*
4. Level **four** communication is *sharing feelings*, including emotions, values and passions.
5. Level **five** is peak communication involving the *sharing of deep intimacy issues*, closet confessions, significant mistakes, shame and abuse.[14]

The skilled coach must know the levels of sharing that are appropriate for a coaching relationship based upon the length of the relationship and the depth of trust established. The wise coach asks questions that typically elicit answers on the appropriate communication level. Asking questions that go beyond the trust levels can be damaging to a coaching relationship.

CONNECTING AT A DEEP LEVEL BY BUILDING TRUST

Spending time together is one good way of developing trust. Another way is sharing some of your life stories—past, present, and future. One observer has stated that sharing his own story and seeing the other person listen with obvious interest is a good way of deepening the bonds of trust with that person.

Start Each Session with a Check-In.
Trust comes easier once people get to know each other. We get to know others by hearing their stories and by sharing our stories. Start each coaching conversation with a brief check-in where the client shares significant things that have happened in his or her life since you last talked. While coaching is all about the client, it will be helpful for the new client to get to know you so briefly share something important that you have experienced lately as well.

One coach was so excited over the project his client was involved in that he chose to ignore the connect phase and jumped right into the topic that was carried over from the previous session. His client discussed the issues and came up with several options to deal with the most pressing ones. He then decided on the next steps he would need to take. The coach enthusiastically asked him, "How likely is it that you can accomplish these first two steps before we talk again next week?" The client replied, "It's not likely at all. In fact, there is zero chance of me getting to any of this in the next couple of weeks!" Bewildered, the coach inquired as to the reason. The coach was dismayed to hear his client say that the client's wife had been hospitalized and had had emergency surgery two days ago. He told the coach that he would be home caring for her over the next couple of weeks. The coach regretted having neglected the connect phase and not discovering this vital information about his client.[15]

Listen Deeply, Without Interrupting.
Listening at a deep level demonstrates respect. It is one way to say, "I really care about you." When someone interrupts the person talking, it suggests one of several things:

- *Indifference*: "What you have been saying is not very important to me."
- *Priority*: "What I am about to say is more important than what you are saying."
- *Arrogance*: "I don't really care what your ideas are on this subject."
- *Superiority*: "I have a lot of wisdom to share, so you should be quiet and listen."
- *Lack of Trust*: "What you are bringing up I'm not comfortable hearing."
- *Impatience*: "This is something we already know, and I want to move on."

Demonstrate Respect by Honoring the Client's Perspectives, Feelings and Opinions.
Everyone has a right to their own viewpoints. You have arrived at your opinions through a unique set of experiences, study, and reasoning. It may be that the client has arrived at his or her outlook through facing difficult life circumstances, so respect their point of view.

THE OBJECTIVE OF THE CONNECT PHASE

The purpose of the connect phase in the CHRISP model is to build trust and rapport. Little can be accomplished in a coaching relationship without having significant trust between coach and client. The connect phase need not be lengthy—perhaps three or four minutes for a sixty-minute appointment.

Sample *Connect* Questions

Here are some questions that can be asked in the connect phase.

- How are you?
- How have you been?
- How are you checking in today?
- What's been going on in your life since we last talked?
- What's happened of significance between our last appointment and today?
- What insights have come to you since our last conversation?

SUMMARY

The connect phase in the CHRISP coaching model serves to establish rapport at the beginning of a coaching conversation and to build trust in the relationship. Connecting need not take long—perhaps just three or four minutes—but it is essential to create trust and to uncover things of importance that have happened in the client's life. Creating an expectation for a check-in at the beginning of each coaching conversation will be very fruitful for your coaching relationships.

4

Phase 2: H = Homework

THE SECOND PHASE OF the CHRISP coaching model is *homework*. Homework is simply reviewing the action steps that the client agreed upon in the last or in recent sessions. Homework relates to the ICF Core Competency 8, Facilitates Client Growth.[16]

Why Homework? Inquiring about the client's progress on action steps is important for accountability. Doing so allows the coach to celebrate victories with the client. It also provides a learning experience for uncovering what obstacles and roadblocks may have prevented the client from completing the action steps. The client knows that the coach will be asking about progress on his or her action steps. This is a powerful motivator for the client to complete action steps and move forward.

This is a natural place in the coaching conversation to inquire about agreed-upon action steps. These steps were formulated toward the end of the previous coaching session, and now, near the beginning of the next session, it is logical to bring up the subject. Knowing whether the client completed the agreed-upon action steps can be essential to understanding how to proceed in the present conversation.

If the client has completed the agreed-upon actions, it is time to celebrate! Ask the client how they would like to celebrate. Perhaps it's only to acknowledge, "I did well!" Or perhaps it's to go to a fancy restaurant for dinner. Big wins call for bigger celebrations!

LEARN FROM FAILURES

Failure to carry through on agreed-upon actions presents a good time for learning. What were those things that kept the client from accomplishing them?

Taking on too much

- The client tried to take on too much on this occasion, so it would make sense to break the project up into smaller pieces.
- The client consistently takes on more than can be done in the time available, so it would be important to explore what causes the client to do so.
- The client took on too much in order to please the coach. Again, this deserves careful discussion.

Priorities and Values
It may be that an uncompleted action step demonstrates that the action was not really important to the client. Such a situation reveals information about the client's values and priorities, and so could result in good learning and self-discovery for the client.

Life Got in the Way

- Perhaps unexpected things happened in the client's life that prevented the client from being able to do the action steps.

Whatever the reason, uncompleted action steps provide fertile ground for discussion with the client to learn and grow. While the coach is firm and resolute in inquiring about forward progress, it is essential for the coach to leave responsibility with the client. The coach does not take on a parental role, nor a judgmental or condemning attitude. Rather, the coach continues to be supportive and encouraging toward the client.

SUMMARY

Homework is simply reviewing the action steps that the client agreed to do in the last or in recent sessions. In most cases, the homework phase is brief, needing only two or three minutes to get a progress update on the client's action steps. While it is brief, the homework phase is essential because it provides accountability and the motivation for the client to complete action steps, and thus make forward progress.

5

Phase 3: R = Result

THE THIRD PHASE OF the CHRISP coaching model is *result*. Result relates closely with the ICF Core Competency 2, Establishes and Maintains Agreements.[17]

Coaching is having an intentional conversation. Each coaching conversation accomplishes the most for the client when there is a purpose and a goal for that conversation. The result phase gives the coach direction. It provides a target for which both coach and client are shooting. If the result phase is not clearly spelled out, the coach is doing nothing more than just having a friendly conversation. For this reason, the coach may need to be more assertive in guiding the conversation here than in any other phase. The coach takes several steps in nailing down the result desired by the client.

GET THE BIG PICTURE

Start by asking a general question that sets the direction for the conversation. Such questions might be:

- Where shall we focus our conversation today?
- What's most important for us to work on today?
- What would make today's conversation most meaningful for you?

- What would be most helpful for us to focus on today?
- What's on your mind today?

NARROW THE FOCUS

Often the subject the client introduces is very broad. The focus must be narrowed so that it is manageable for the time allotted. The coach might do this by asking:

- What result would you like to take away from our conversation today?
- What can we accomplish that would be meaningful for you this session?
- What do you want to have at the end of this conversation that you don't have now?

ESTABLISH MEASURABILITY

It is important for the coach to know how to measure success for the conversation, since this provides specific direction for the coach. Measurement often involves numbers, while at other times it is more difficult to define. These questions might help:

- How can we measure success for this conversation?
- How will we know that we have accomplished what we set out to do?
- What would success look like for today's session?

UNDERSTAND MOTIVATIONS AND CIRCUMSTANCES

Understanding why the client chose the topic they did can be very helpful for the coach. Perhaps the client is facing a difficult choice or has experienced a crisis in his or her life. It's helpful for the coach to know what causes the client to bring up a particular issue at that time. Revealing questions might be:

- What makes this issue most important for us to talk about in this session?
- What's happening in your life that brings this issue to the surface today?
- Of all the dozens of things we could talk about, what makes you decide to focus on this one for today?
- Why this topic for today?

UNCOVER POINTS TO ADDRESS

The client probably has already given the issue some careful thought. In his or her mind, there likely are various aspects to be addressed or things to be resolved. By uncovering these various points, the coach is having the client set forth an agenda for the conversation. The coach might ask:

- What are the various points to this issue that we should cover?
- What issues must be resolved as we focus on this?
- What are the key things we should be sure to talk about?

FEEDBACK FOR CLARIFICATION

Once the coach has discussed the results the client wants out of the conversation, the coach summarizes and paraphrases what the client wants to accomplish, how it will be measured, why it is important to the client, and the various points to be covered. After the client affirms the coach's summary, the coach might ask, "Where's a good place to jump into this issue?" The client likely knows better than the coach where to begin, and this is a good way to partner with the client.

BE THOROUGH—TAKE YOUR TIME!

Beginning coaches often want to rush through the result phase so they can get to the "real" aspect of coaching. This is a mistake! Without knowing the various points covered above, the coach will be ill-prepared to guide the coaching conversation. While fledgling coaches sometime think three minutes is taking too long, masterful coaches often spend fifteen minutes or more uncovering all the treasures in the result phase.

During one coaching conversation with a leader, we took twenty minutes for the result phase. After summarizing what he wanted to accomplish, I asked him where he would like to jump into the issue. He startled me by saying, "Nowhere." Confused, I asked him what he meant. He replied, "I've gotten what I came for. I already have my answer. We don't need to talk anymore. I've resolved the issue in my mind already." We concluded that coaching session early because of the power of the result phase.

SUMMARY

Each coaching conversation is an intentional one with a specific focus. The coach best serves the client by establishing a purpose and a goal for that conversation. The result phase gives the coach direction. It provides a target for which both coach and client are shooting. A thorough result phase will reveal what the client wants to accomplish, how it will be measured, why the issue is important to the client, and the various points to be covered.

6

Phase 4: I = Investigate

THE FOURTH PHASE IN the CHRISP coaching model is *investigate*. Investigate relates to several of the ICF core competencies, including # 5, Maintains Presence, # 6, Listens Actively, and # 7, Evokes Awareness.[18]

The investigate phase occupies the largest segment in a coaching conversation. In the typical beginning coach's mind, this is the "real" part of coaching. In reality, however, all phases of the coaching model are real coaching. In a sixty-minute coaching conversation, the investigate phase typically occupies thirty-five to forty minutes of the time.

The investigate phase is the least clearly defined and the most open-ended of all the phases. Here is where the coach most obviously "dances"with the client, as the client takes the lead and the coach follows. The coach supports the client in the investigate phase by using active listening, by asking good questions, and by occasionally sharing observations about the client.

ACTIVE LISTENING

As we consider listening, let's look at the various levels of listening. (For an expanded discussion of listening skills see chapter 15.)

- *Non-Listening* includes daydreaming, internal listening, argumentative listening, and therapeutic listening.
- *Beginning listening* incorporates posture, silence, grunts, door openers, and parroting.
- *Intermediate listening* involves summarizing and paraphrasing.
- *Advanced listening* includes empathetic listening and 360 degree listening.
- *Masterful listening* means listening on many levels at the same time.

POWERFUL QUESTIONING

Questions have amazing power. Questions automatically start us looking. Questions can jolt people awake. Questions can stimulate new ideas. Questions can open eyes to see new places and new ways of doing things. Chad Holliday, former chairman of the board and CEO of Dupont, once said, "I find that when someone engages me in a question, it wakes me up. I'm in a different place."[19] (For an expanded discussion of asking powerful questions see chapter 18.)

Asking a question rather than giving an order isn't just polite, it's smart. Here are a few reasons why:

- Questions draw out the other person's thinking, ideas, and perspectives.
- Questions increase ownership–the answers are theirs.
- Questions may produce new learning—for them and for you.
- Questions show respect for their ideas, thinking, and them as people.

- Beginning with a question makes a powerful statement about your trust and respect for the person and creates greater openness to your input.

QUESTIONS THAT ARE NOT POWERFUL

If you want to ask powerful questions, avoid these types of questions: closed questions, leading questions, punishing questions, information-gathering questions, directive questions, run-on questions, and stacked questions.

Closed questions can be answered with just one word and they shut down conversation.

Leading questions are manipulative statements with a phrase tacked on to turn it into a question.

Punishing questions put the other person on the spot and judges their motives.

Information-gathering questions have a narrow focus as they probe for more facts and details.

Directive questions contain a subtle suggestion for what the client should do.

Run-on or complicated questions use a great many words and so are confusing to understand.

Stacked questions happen when the coach asks several questions at once before giving a chance for the client to reply.

FORMING POWERFUL QUESTIONS

If you want to ask powerful questions, keep these things in mind.

The Purpose of Questions = A New Perspective
Coaching questions are not meant to garner more information from the client but instead to prompt the client to think, feel, or react differently about the issue. A coach who focuses on the technical details of a client's specific problem does so at the risk of becoming a prisoner to the same limiting frame of reference as the client. Instead, the coach explores the general framework that underlies the way the client has looked at an issue and the way the client has searched for solutions. This change of perspective on goals and issues is what will enable the client to suddenly discover totally new approaches in defining and solving the problem.

Coaches who do not know how to ask the right coaching question tend to elicit more and more information from clients with content-oriented questions. In doing so they not only unknowingly reinforce their client's restrictive perspective, but they themselves risk getting stuck having a limited perspective that prevents seeing viable solutions. Therefore, a correct coaching attitude consists of journeying with the client but without getting sucked into that person's underlying frame of reference and mindset. A coach helps a client to question their viewpoint and to perceive their situation from a new angle. Powerful coaching questions are those that transform the client's frame of reference and allow them to see things from a new perspective. When we ask a powerful question, the intent is to help a client look deeper and find possible answers from a new perspective rather than continuing to respond from an old, familiar place.

How do you know that you've asked a powerful question? Often there will be moments of significant silence as the client considers the implications of the question. Perhaps the person will say, "Wow! I never thought of it in that way before."

THE SHIFT

In working with a client, a shift is something for which the coach hopes. A shift happens when a client sees an issue from a new perspective. The coach's questions and occasional feedback can help a client see things in a new light. Suddenly a shift occurs, and the "light" goes on.

Perhaps you are familiar with Sudoku puzzles. The object of Sudoku is to fill in a grid of missing numbers following specific rules for each row, column, and box. Some of the puzzle is already filled in. At times, it may seem that the puzzle cannot be solved, if using only one or two of the rules. However, to successfully solve the puzzle one has to look at it from at least three different points of view – the columns, the rows, and each of the larger squares. In looking at the puzzle from different angles, often one gets a different perspective, and the light goes on! There is a sudden shift, and the puzzle is solved!

Think of a world map. Many maps intended for Western audiences show North and South America in the center. However, another valid point of view is with Australia and Asia in the center. A striking option that is just as accurate is seeing the world from the point of view from the North Pole! Each version shows the same continents, but provides the viewer with an entirely different perspective on the world.

In a coaching conversation, the coach asks questions about the issue from various angles. These questions help a client see the "puzzle" from a different angle. Suddenly they get a new perspective and there is a shift in their thinking!

SHARING OBSERVATIONS

Frequently, the coach will notice significant things about the client or about the client's situation. At times the client is not aware of this, so it can be very helpful to the client for the coach to make observations. This is called direction communication. However, sharing observations is often where beginning coaches can get into trouble, so use it sparingly. Limit your observations to what you are noticing in the client at that moment or about what you are seeing in the client's situation. The coach might say, "I'm noticing that you appear to be quite upset." Or, "It seems that your situation is extremely complicated."

SUMMARY

The investigate phase occupies the largest segment in a coaching conversation. It is the least clearly defined and the most open-ended of all the phases. The coach supports the client in the investigate phase by using active listening, by asking good questions, and by occasionally reflecting back in sharing observations with the client. Ideally, in the investigate phase the issue the client brought up has been explored and the desired result has been achieved. The investigate phase naturally leads to creating action steps.

7

Phase 5: S = Steps

THE FIFTH PHASE IN the CHRISP coaching model is that of *steps*. Steps refers to action steps or homework the client decides to take to move forward. The steps phase relates to the ICF Core Competency 7, Evokes Awareness.[20]

WHY ACTION STEPS?

Action steps arise out of the investigate phase of the coaching conversation. Action steps help solidify learning for the client. Action steps are a logical necessity as a result of the issue the client has raised. If the coach has done well in working with the client through the investigate phase, typically the actions to be taken by the client will be very apparent.

How are action steps determined? Beginning coaches sometimes have the mindset that they are to assign homework to the client. More experienced coaches have learned the value of clients creating their own action steps because then they then own them and are more likely to follow through in doing them.

A SIMPLE QUESTION

Here is a simple non-threatening and open question that helps clients design actions: *What actions could you take to move forward?*[21] It's simple but powerful. Look at how this question is constructed.

- *What* — Beginning with an open question makes people think.
- *actions* — Asking for multiple actions will spawn deeper thinking and invite greater creativity.
- *could you take* — Saying *could*, rather than *will* takes some pressure off and encourages more options.
- *to move forward?* — Saying *move forward* allows for a process, for next steps, and for partial completion. Even a little step is forward progress. This wording expects progress without requiring that everything is to be accomplished all at once.

The coach can direct the client to a specific area for action by adding the context to the end of the question. Such as: *What actions could you take to move forward on this issue?*

MAKE IT SMART

If the action step is quite significant or is likely to take some time to accomplish, the coach might help the client in making sure that the intended action is SMART (Specific, Measurable, Achievable, Relevant, and Timebound). After writing the initial goal or action step, add a "so that" phrase because this forces the client to think through what he or she is really after.

ENSURE FOLLOW-THROUGH

Once your client decides on the action step, there still is more work to be done to ensure follow-through. Your client will need support to overcome obstacles and be held accountable.

Support. The coach can ask questions such as:

- What support do you need to carry out this action step?
- What resources would be helpful in following through on this?
- Where can you find those resources?

Obstacles. The coach can ask:

- What might keep you from following through with this action step?
- How can you prevent that from sidelining you?

Accountability. The coach can ask:

- What accountability structures would be helpful in carrying out this action step?
- Who can you ask to hold you accountable for this action step?
- On a scale of 1 to 10, how likely is it that you actually will get this done?

SUMMARY

The fifth phase in the CHRISP coaching model is that of *steps*, referring to action steps or homework the client decides to take to move forward. Action steps arise out of the coaching conversation and, if the investigate phase has gone well, are typically very apparent. Action steps are needed to help solidify learning for the client. The simple question, *What actions could you take to move forward?* will help the client formulate the needed steps.

8

Phase 6: P = Purpose

THE SIXTH AND FINAL phase of the CHRISP coaching model is *purpose*. This phase refers to the ICF Core Competency 7, Evokes Awareness and Competency 8, Facilitates Client Growth.[22]

THE IMPORTANCE OF THE PURPOSE PHASE

This phase is much greater than simply asking, "To what extent did we accomplish our purpose for today's session?" The purpose phase is essential for several reasons:

- It confirms that coach and client have accomplished what they set out to do in the result phase.
- It helps cement the learning that has occurred for the client during the coaching conversation.
- It allows the coach to draw attention to both new insights the client has received about the presenting situation as well as new insights about him or herself.
- It provides the opportunity to extend the learning to a broader scope in the client's life, not just the immediate presenting issue.
- It can highlight "aha" moments when new perspectives were gained and perhaps a shift occurred for the

client. In doing this, the possibility of transformation and growth in the client's life is reinforced.

- It allows the coach to partner with the client in closing the session.

ASPECTS OF THE PURPOSE PHASE

There are several clear parts to the purpose phase.

Confirm the Result. Early in the purpose phase is a good time to make sure that the result the client wanted for the session has been accomplished. There are several ways to inquire.

- How well have we done in accomplishing what we set out to do?
- To what extent have you gotten what you had hoped for?
- How well have we succeeded in reaching the goal we aimed for at the beginning of our conversation?

Inquire about various things learned. Specifically, the coach is interested in knowing what the client learned about the presenting issue, in new insights gained about oneself, and how the client might apply these new things learned to other aspects of his or her life.

- What has been most useful to you in our conversation today?
- What has become clear to you regarding the issue we covered today?
- What insights may have come to you about yourself?
- What have you learned that you can apply to other areas of your life?

- How will your life be different six months from now because we had this conversation today?

I was coaching a busy executive who was concerned that family responsibilities were keeping him from accomplishing certain goals. I asked questions that invited him to evaluate how the demands on his time lined up with his long-term values. As the conversation drew to a close, I asked him what value he had gotten from our time together. He surprised me with this insight. "I've come to the realization that I need to always ask myself this question, using it as a grid to evaluate my activities: 'Is this activity moving me toward having more impact on people or away from it?'"

Commend the client for the work done today. Say something like "You've done good work today." Or "I appreciate the way you have focused and really applied yourself in this session."

Affirm the client's overall progress. This may be a good time for the coach to reflect on the progress the client has made over the past several weeks or months. Affirming the progress encourages the client to keep moving forward, and it also strengthens the bond in the relationship.

Confirm the date and time of the next appointment. In light of clients' busy schedules, it is a good idea to schedule appointments several months ahead. At this point in the conversation, it is helpful to make sure you are both clear on the next date and time to talk, including how or where the session will be held.

Partner with the client to close the session. Masterful coaches see the coaching relationship as a partnership, so they continually look for ways they can partner with the client. The purpose phase is a good place to do this. Rather than looking at the clock and conveying to the client that the time is up, consider a more effective way. Say something like: "What else we should talk about to make this conversation complete for you before we wrap up?"

SUMMARY

The purpose phase is last, but certainly not least, in the coaching conversation. This is the opportunity to make sure the desired goal was met, to highlight new insights about the situation and oneself, to broaden the learning to all of life, to commend the client for good work done, to confirm the next appointment, and to close the session graciously. The purpose phase should put an exclamation point on the conversation for the client.

SECTION III

The ICF Core Competencies

9

Overview of the ICF Core Competencies

COACHING IS A RELATIVE newcomer among the various approaches of helping people. As a profession, coaching is still young, having emerged during the 1980s. In spite of its youthfulness, coaching has become widely accepted because of its effectiveness in helping people achieve their goals and dreams. In the corporate world, coaching, along with mentoring and consulting, has emerged as a preeminent way to achieve professional growth,

THE INTERNATIONAL COACHING FEDERATION

It is estimated that today there are approximately 110,000 coaches worldwide, of which about 99,000 are active practitioners. Several organizations have arisen to provide support and guidance to those coaches. The largest of these is the International Coaching Federation (ICF), with more than 57,563 members and 141 chapters in 99 countries. As of February 2023, there are 49,970 coaches who hold one of three ICF credentials:

- 26,563 Associate Certified Coaches (ACC);
- 21,348 Professional Certified Coaches (PCC);
- 2,059 Master Certified Coaches (MCC).

Roughly 40% of members come from North America. Regarding age distribution, 48% of coaches worldwide are Gen Xers; 42% are Baby Boomers; and 10% are Millennials. Regarding gender, 72% of coaches worldwide are female. When it comes to education, only 5% of coaches do not have a college degree. In fact, 65% have either a master's or a doctoral degree.[23]

Other coaching organizations include the Association of Coaches (IAC); the Center for Credentialing and Education (CCE) that offers the BCC credential (Board Certified Coach); the European Mentoring and Coaching Council (EMCC); and the Christian Coaches Network International (CCNI). Without question, the ICF is the largest and most influential coaching organization. Eighty-six percent of coaches world-wide belong to one of these coaching organizations, and 85% of all coaches hold a credential from a coaching organization.

In 2020, its twenty-fifth anniversary year, ICF became the International Coaching Federation (instead of the International Coach Federation) and transitioned from a single organization to a federation of six family organizations:

- ICF Coaching in Organizations,
- ICF Coach Training,
- ICF Credentials and Standards,
- ICF Foundation,
- ICF Professional Coaches
- ICF Thought Leadership.

THE CORE COMPETENCIES OF THE ICF

The International Coaching Federation is committed to maintaining and promoting excellence in coaching. To this end, the ICF has developed eight core competencies that help to guide coaches in their development as skillful coaches. These core coaching competencies were developed to support greater understanding about the skills and approaches used within today's coaching profession, as defined by the International Coaching Federation. They serve as a guide both for individual coaches seeking to elevate their coaching skills and for students attending schools that provide coaching training to acquire an ICF credential.

THE ORIGINAL ELEVEN CORE COMPETENCIES

The development of the core competencies makes for a fascinating story. In 1998, just three years following the founding of the ICF, eight experienced coaches came together to define the fundamental competencies that a professional coach should demonstrate. Each of these eight were directors of a coaching school or a department of coaching at a university. The schools represented were the Hudson Institute, Newfield Network, Coaches Training Institute, Coach U, Coach for Life, Success Unlimited Network, Academy of Coach Training, and New Ventures West. They sought to elevate the credibility of the coaching profession by creating guidelines for coach training and defining requirements for coach certification.

The result of these eight coaches' collaboration became the eleven core competencies of the International Coach Federation. The core competencies were grouped into four clusters according to those that fit together logically, based on common ways of looking at the competencies in each group. A brief description is provided below for each competency.[24]

A. SETTING THE FOUNDATION

1. **Meeting Ethical Guidelines and Professional Standards**—Understanding of coaching ethics and standards and ability to apply them appropriately in all coaching situations.
   Understands and exhibits in own behaviors the ICF Code of Ethics.

2. **Establishing the Coaching Agreement**—Ability to understand what is required in the specific coaching interaction and to come to agreement with the prospective and new client about the coaching process and relationship.

B. CO-CREATING THE RELATIONSHIP

3. **Establishing Trust and Intimacy with the Client**—Ability to create a safe, supportive environment that produces ongoing mutual respect and trust.

4. **Coaching Presence**—Ability to be fully conscious and create a spontaneous relationship with the client, employing a style that is open, flexible, and confident.

C. COMMUNICATING EFFECTIVELY

5. **Active Listening**—Ability to focus completely on what the client is saying and is not saying, to understand the meaning of what is said in the context of the client's desires, and to support client self-expression.

6. **Powerful Questioning**—Ability to ask questions that reveal the information needed for maximum benefit to the coaching relationship and the client.

7. **Direct Communication**—Ability to communicate effectively during coaching sessions, and to use language that has the greatest positive impact on the client.

D. FACILITATING LEARNING AND RESULTS

8. **Creating Awareness**—Ability to integrate and accurately evaluate multiple sources of information and to make interpretations that help the client to gain awareness and thereby achieve agreed-upon results.

9. **Designing Actions**—Ability to create with the client opportunities for ongoing learning, during coaching and in work/life situations, and for taking new actions that will most effectively lead to agreed-upon coaching results.

10. **Planning and Goal Setting**—Ability to develop and maintain an effective coaching plan with the client.

11. **Managing Progress and Accountability**—Ability to hold attention on what is important for the client and to leave responsibility with the client to take action.

THE UPDATED EIGHT CORE COMPETENCIES

An updated version of the core competencies was introduced in October 2019. A rigorous, twenty-four-month coaching practice analysis was used to collect data from more than thirteen hundred coaches across the world. These coaches represented a diverse range of coaching disciplines, training backgrounds, coaching styles, and experience levels, including both ICF members and non-members. The research project validated much of the original core competencies, but it also surfaced several new elements that were integrated into the eight competencies. These include:

- Emphasis on ethical behavior and confidentiality
- Importance of a coaching mindset and ongoing reflective practice
- Distinctions between coaching agreements
- Importance of partnership between coach and client
- Awareness of cultural, systemic, and contextual factors

The revised eight core competencies are listed here, with definitions.[25]

1. DEMONSTRATES ETHICAL PRACTICE

Definition: *Understands and consistently applies coaching ethics and standards of coaching.*

2. EMBODIES A COACHING MINDSET

Definition: *Develops and maintains a mindset that is open, curious, flexible, and client centered.*

3. ESTABLISHES AND MAINTAINS AGREEMENTS

Definition: *Partners with the client and relevant stakeholders to create clear agreements about the coaching relationship, process, plans, and goals. Establishes agreements for the overall coaching engagement as well as those for each coaching session.*

4. CULTIVATES TRUST AND SAFETY

Definition: *Partners with the client to create a safe, supportive environment that allows the client to share freely. Maintains a relationship of mutual respect and trust.*

5. MAINTAINS PRESENCE

Definition: *Is fully conscious and present with the client, employing a style that is open, flexible, grounded, and confident.*

6. LISTENS ACTIVELY

Definition: *Focuses on what the client is and is not saying to fully understand what is being communicated in the context of the client systems and to support client self-expression.*

7. EVOKES AWARENESS

Definition: *Facilitates client insight and learning by using tools and techniques such as powerful questioning, silence, metaphor, or analogy.*

8. FACILITATES CLIENT GROWTH

Definition: *Partners with the client to transform learning and insight into action. Promotes client autonomy in the coaching process.*

THE THREE CREDENTIALS OF THE ICF

The International Coaching Federation has established three levels of credentialing. Each credential represents an increasing skill level for a coach, as well as increased hours of study and experience. Here is a summary of the credentials and some requirements.[26]

Credential	Stands For	Coach-Specific Training Hours Required	Coaching Hours Required
ACC	Associate Certified Coach	60	100
PCC	Professional Certified Coach	125	500
MCC	Master Certified Coach	200	2,500

10

Demonstrates Ethical Practice

ICF Core Competency 1

THE INTERNATIONAL COACHING FEDERATION is committed to maintaining and promoting excellence in coaching. All ICF members and credentialed coaches are expected to adhere to ethical conduct, as well as to integrate the ICF core competencies effectively in their work. The *Code of Ethics* is designed to provide appropriate guidelines, accountability, and enforceable standards of conduct for all ICF members and ICF credential holders.[27]

The ICF defines the first core competency as the coach understands and consistently applies coaching ethics and standards of coaching. [28]

When applying coaching ethics and standards, the coach . . .

1. Demonstrates personal integrity and honesty in interactions with clients, sponsors, and relevant stakeholders.
2. Is sensitive to clients' identity, environment, experiences, values, and beliefs.
3. Uses language appropriate and respectful to clients, sponsors, and relevant stakeholders

4. Abides by the ICF Code of Ethics and upholds the Core Values.
5. Maintains confidentiality with client information per stakeholder agreements and pertinent laws.
6. Maintains the distinctions between coaching, consulting, psychotherapy, and other support professions.
7. Refers clients to other support professionals, as appropriate.[29]

Familiarity with the ICF Code of Ethics and its application is required for all levels of coaching, and the standard for demonstrating a strong ethical understanding of coaching is similar for an ICF credential at any level—Associate Certified Coach (ACC), Professional Certified Coach (PCC) or Master Certified Coach (MCC).

An applicant must demonstrate alignment with the ICF Code of Ethics in the performance evaluation. An applicant who commits a clear violation of the ICF Code of Ethics within a performance evaluation would not pass this competency and would be denied certification.

An applicant must also remain consistently in the role of coach within the performance evaluation. This includes demonstrating a knowledge of the coaching conversation that is focused on inquiry and exploration, and a focus based on present and future issues. An applicant would not pass this competency if they focus primarily on telling the client what to do or how to do it (consulting mode) or if the conversation is based primarily in the past, particularly the emotional past (therapeutic mode).

If an applicant doesn't have a basic understanding of the skills that underlie the ICF definition of coaching, that lack of comprehension will be reflected in other competencies listed below. For example, if a coach almost exclusively gives advice or indicates that a particular answer chosen by the coach is what the client should do, trust and safety, presence, active listening, evoking awareness, and facilitating client growth will not be present and a credential at any level would be denied.[30]

OVERVIEW OF RESOURCES

A complete overview of ICF's thought on ethical coaching can be obtained by reading these three key documents on the ICF website:

- Code of Ethics
- ICF Standards for Ethical Conduct
- Interpretive Statements

The ICF Code of Ethics and Standards may be found at this link:

https://coachingfederation.org/ethics/code-of-ethics

The Interpretive Statements on the Standards may be found at this link:

https://coachfederation.org/interpretive-statements

OUTLINE OF CODE OF ETHICS

The ICF Code of Ethics has five divisions.

1. Introduction
2. Key Definitions
3. Core Values and Ethical Principles
4. Ethical Standards
5. Pledge

CORE VALUES

The core values of the ICF include professionalism, collaboration, humanity and equity.

1. *Professionalism*: We commit to a coaching mindset and professional quality that encompasses responsibility, respect, integrity, competence and excellence.
2. *Collaboration*: We commit to develop social connection and community building.
3. *Humanity:* We commit to being humane, kind, compassionate and respectful toward others.
4. *Equity:* We commit to use a coaching mindset to explore and understand the needs of others so we can practice equitable processes at all times that create equality for all.

ETHICAL STANDARDS

According to the ethical standards, a coach's responsibilities lie in these areas:[31]

- Responsibilities to *Clients*
- Responsibilities to *Practice and Performance*
- Responsibilities to *Professionalism*
- Responsibilities to *Society*

RESPONSIBILITIES TO *CLIENTS*

A coach's responsibilities to clients include these essentials.

- At an initial meeting, explaining the nature of coaching, confidentiality, and its limits, financial arrangements, and terms of the coaching agreement.
- Creating an agreement or contract detailing the roles, responsibilities and rights of all parties involved, including clients and sponsors.
- Managing potential conflicts of interest through the coaching agreement and ongoing dialogue.
- Properly maintaining, storing, and disposing of coaching records, including electronic files and communication, in a way that promotes confidentiality and privacy.
- Being aware of a shift in value from the coaching relationship and respecting the right of all parties to terminate the coaching relationship at any time for any reason.
- Being aware of any power or status difference due to cultural, relational, psychological, or contextual issues.
- Assuring consistent quality of coaching regardless of the amount or form of agreed compensation.

RESPONSIBILITIES TO *PRACTICE AND PERFORMANCE*

- Commitment to excellence through continued personal, professional, and ethical development.
- Recognizing personal limitations or circumstances that may impair, conflict with or interfere with coaching performance.
- Resolving conflicts by working through the issue, seeking professional assistance, or ending the professional relationship.
- Maintaining the privacy of ICF Members and use the ICF Member contact information only in authorized ways.

RESPONSIBILITIES TO *PROFESSIONALISM*

- Identifying accurately my coaching qualifications, my level of coaching competency, expertise, experience, training, certifications and ICF credentials.
- Making verbal and written statements that are true and accurate about what I offer as an ICF Professional, and the potential value of coaching.
- Setting clear, appropriate and culturally sensitive boundaries that govern interactions, physical or otherwise.
- Avoiding any sexual or romantic engagement with clients or sponsors, and being mindful of the level of intimacy appropriate for the relationship.

RESPONSIBILITIES TO *SOCIETY*

- Maintaining fairness and equality in all activities and operations, while respecting local rules and cultural practices. This includes not discriminating on the basis of age, race, gender expression, ethnicity, sexual orientation, religion, national origin, disability, or military status.
- Honoring the intellectual property of others, only claiming ownership of my own material.
- Being aware of impact on society, and adhering to the philosophy of "doing good" versus "avoiding bad."

THREE ESSENTIAL FOCAL POINTS

Dr. Frances Penafort, MCC, was a member of the team that presented the updated 2019 Code of Ethics, as well as being on the Internal Review Board (IRB) that reviews complaints brought against coaches. In the YouTube video "Updated ICF Core Competency 1: Demonstrates Ethical Practice," Dr. Penafort declares that ethical practice is the foundation upon which a person comes to a coaching relationship. She suggests that three focal points are required in order to demonstrate ethical practice:

- Focus on *myself* – "Am I bringing professionalism, honesty, and integrity?"
- Focus on the *relationship* – "Am I being kind, considerate, and respectful?"
- Focus on the *system* – "Am I representing the ICF and its Code of Ethics well?"[32]

WHAT IS REQUIRED

- An understanding of coaching ethics and standards.
- The ability to apply ethics and standards appropriately in all coaching situations.

This means . . .

- The coach understands and exhibits in his/her own behaviors the ICF Code of Ethics.
- The coach understands and follows all ICF Ethical Guidelines.
- The coach clearly communicates the distinctions between coaching, consulting, psychotherapy, and other support professions.
- The coach knows when a client needs other professional help and refers the client to available resources.

An applicant will not pass this competency if . . .

- The coach focuses primarily on telling the client what to do or how to do it (consulting mode).
- The conversation is based primarily in the past, particularly the emotional past (therapeutic mode).
- The coach is not clear on basic foundation exploration and evoking skills that underlie the ICF definition of coaching.
- The coach clearly does not have the skills to cultivate trust and safety, maintain presence, ask powerful questions, listen actively, evoke awareness, and generate client actions and accountability.

HOW TO AVOID THE MISTAKES OTHER COACHES HAVE MADE

Some coaches have committed blunders that caused them to appear in a court of law or to appear before the ICF Internal Review Board (IRB) with the threat of their credential being revoked. To avoid getting in trouble, be sure to follow these six steps that were shared with me by Dr. Michael Marx, MCC and a member of the IRB (Internal Review Board).

1. *Be clear about what you are offering as a coach.* Adhere to the maxim, "under promise and over deliver." Refrain from making claims about the results your clients can expect that you cannot substantiate.
2. *Explain the difference between coaching and other helping approaches.* Clarify with prospective and new clients the differences between coaching, mentoring, consulting, counseling, and therapy.
3. *Don't overstate your coaching qualifications.* Accurately identify your coaching qualifications, expertise, experience, training, certifications, and ICF credentials. Understand the difference between a certificate (a diploma a coaching school may give to you as proof of graduation) and an ICF credential (certification that indicates a certain skill and experience level).
4. *Put agreements in writing.* Have written contracts and agreements that completely spell out the limits and expectations of the coaching agreement.
5. *Recognize your own limitations.* Know when to refer a client to another helping professional. It is your responsibility to not only know when to refer but also to whom to refer. Therefore, you must be acquainted with certain health professionals in your community.

6. *Keep confidentialities.* Don't discuss coaching conversations with others—unless it is your coach supervisor. Mentioning to someone that you are coaching so and so is a violation of the Code of Ethics.[33]

SUMMARY

Excellence in coaching is reflected in the high standards of conduct set forth in the ICF's Code of Ethics. While it is listed as the first core competency of the ICF, the Code of Ethics is not so much a skill as it is a mindset, an attitude, and a way of conducting oneself at a high professional level. The ICF Code of Ethics safeguards the coaching profession, as well as protects individual coaches who adhere to its standards.

11

Embodies a Coaching Mindset

ICF Core Competency 2

THE INTERNATIONAL COACHING FEDERATION defines a coaching mindset as one in which the coach develops and maintains a mindset that is open, curious, flexible, and client centered.

When having a coaching mindset, the coach . . .

1. Acknowledges that clients are responsible for their own choices.
2. Engages in ongoing learning and development as a coach.
3. Develops an ongoing reflective practice to enhance one's coaching.
4. Remains aware of and open to the influence of context and culture on self and others.
5. Uses awareness of self and one's intuition to benefit clients.
6. Develops and maintains the ability to regulate one's emotions.
7. Mentally and emotionally prepares for sessions.
8. Seeks help from outside sources when necessary[34]

Embodies a Coaching Mindset serves as a foundational competency for coach practitioners, focused primarily on the "being" of the coach. The related behaviors are typically demonstrated across a coach's practice, more so than in any specific coaching session. This competency area is therefore more difficult to consistently assess within the performance evaluation process. As a result, there are no behavioral or skill statements in this Competency area that are used for assessment purposes. Rather, an applicant's knowledge of and ability to apply Embodies a Coaching Mindset is more directly evaluated in the ICF Credentialing written exam.

THE PCC MARKERS

A team of experienced coaches created the PCC markers. The original PCC markers were first presented in May 2014. With the revision of the core competencies in November 2019, the PCC markers also required revision. This was done in October 2020. These markers can be considered as skills or behaviors at the professional coach skill level. The markers help coaches guide and determine their progress in acquiring coaching skills as they advance.[35] There are eleven markers for Embodies a Coaching Mindset. (Note that the numbers below refer to core competencies 4, 5, 6, and 7.)

4.1: Coach acknowledges and respects the client's unique talents, insights, and work in the coaching process.
4.2: Coach shows support, empathy, or concern for the client.
4.3: Coach acknowledges and supports the client's expression of feelings, perceptions, concerns, beliefs, or suggestions.

4.4: Coach partners with the client by inviting the client to respond in any way to the coach's contributions and accepts the client's response.

5.1: Coach acts in response to the whole person of the client (the who).

5.2: Coach acts in response to what the client wants to accomplish throughout this session (the what).

5.3: Coach partners with the client by supporting the client to choose what happens in this session.

6.1: Coach's questions and observations are customized by using what the coach has learned about who the client is or the client's situation.

6.5: Coach inquires about or explores how the client currently perceives themself or their world.

7.1: Coach asks questions about the client, such as their current way of thinking, feeling, values, needs, wants, beliefs or behavior.

7.5: Coach shares, with no attachment, observations, intuitions, comments, thoughts or feelings, and invites the client's exploration through verbal or tonal invitation. [36]

YOU ARE EMBODYING A COACHING MINDSET WHEN . . .

- *You acknowledge that your clients are responsible for their own choices.*
  You cannot live your clients' lives for them. They make their own choices, and they must live by their choices. You can help them make wise choices, but ultimately you are not responsible for how they live their lives.

- *You engage in ongoing learning and development as a coach.*
  There are numerous ways to grow as a coach. Read books on coaching. Attend coaching seminars and conferences. Take advantage of offerings by your local ICF chapter. Record and analyze your own coaching conversations. Work toward the next ICF coach certification. Employ a coach mentor or a coach supervisor.

- *You develop an ongoing reflective practice to enhance your coaching.*
  Reflect for a few minutes after each coaching conversation and ask yourself questions such as: "What went well? What could I have done better? How could I be more effective as a coach?" Write your answers in a journal and review them from time to time.

- *You remember how much context and culture influence you and your clients.*
  Keep in mind the economic and educational differences that exist between you and your clients. Be aware of what is going on in the cities and countries where they live and how this impacts them.

- *You use your awareness of yourself and your intuition to benefit your clients.*
  Well-developed emotional intelligence is essential to being an effective coach. It is important to be aware of your own emotional state, to be sensitive to the emotions of others, and to be aware of how you are impacting them emotionally. Masterful coaches learn to rely on their intuition and to trust their gut in sensitive situations.

- *You develop the ability to regulate your own emotions.*
  There are times when a client's words or behaviors 'trigger' you emotionally. To serve that client well, you must manage the feelings that arise and stay in a good place emotionally. You learn to be comfortable with a client's strong emotions, such as anger or grief. While you are able to empathize with them, you remain emotionally stable.

- *You prepare well for coaching sessions, both mentally and emotionally.*
  Preparing well for a coaching conversation includes reviewing notes from the previous session, as well as remembering the action steps the client had committed to. Sending questions a few days before the appointment and reviewing the client's responses are important steps in preparation. Preparing well involves getting adequate rest the night before, being in a good frame of mind, setting aside potential distractions, and thinking through the coaching conversation as you anticipate any issues that might arise.

- *You seek help from outside sources, when necessary.*
  Outside sources might be talking with a mentor coach, with a coach supervisor, or with a peer support group. Sources of help might be other professionals, such as a counselor, a psychologist, a pastor or priest, an educational specialist, or a medical physician.

ASSESSOR QUESTIONS

1. Does the coach acknowledge that clients are responsible for their own choices?

2. Does the coach give evidence of engaging in ongoing learning and development as a coach?
3. Does the coach have an ongoing reflective practice to enhance one's coaching?
4. Does the coach demonstrate awareness of the influence of context and culture on self and others?
5. Does the coach use awareness of self and one's intuition to benefit clients?
6. Does the coach appear to regulate one's emotions?
7. Does the coach demonstrate mental and emotional preparedness for session?
8. Does the coach seek help from outside sources when necessary?

SUMMARY

Embodying a coaching mindset means that the coach develops and maintains a mindset that is open, curious, flexible, and client centered. To a great extent, proficiency here means acquiring skills described in the other seven core competencies. These are abilities not acquired overnight but are developed throughout the course of one's coaching career.

12

Establishes and Maintains Agreements

Core Competency 3

IN THIS COMPETENCY THE coach "partners with the client and relevant stakeholders to create clear agreements about the coaching relationship, process, plans, and goals. The coach establishes agreements for the overall coaching engagement as well as those for each coaching session."[37]

The ICF further explains what is involved in fulfilling this competency with these eleven descriptive statements. The coach . . .

1. Explains what coaching is and is not and describes the process to the client and relevant stakeholders.
2. Reaches an agreement about what is and is not appropriate in the relationship, what is and is not being offered, and the responsibilities of the client and relevant stakeholders.
3. Reaches an agreement about the guidelines and specific parameters of the coaching relationship such as logistics, fees, scheduling, duration, termination, confidentiality, and inclusion of others.

4. Partners with the client and relevant stakeholders to establish an overall coaching plan and goals.
5. Partners with the client to determine client-coach compatibility.
6. Partners with the client to identify or reconfirm what they want to accomplish in the session.
7. Partners with the client to define what the client believes they need to address or resolve to achieve what they want to accomplish in the session.
8. Partners with the client to define or reconfirm measures of success for what the client wants to accomplish in the coaching engagement or individual session.
9. Partners with the client to manage the time and focus of the session.
10. Continues coaching in the direction of the client's desired outcome unless the client indicates otherwise.
11. Partners with the client to end the coaching relationship in a way that honors the experience.[38]

Two agreements actually are required. First, the rules of engagement regarding the overall coaching relationship must be created. Note that numbers 1 through 5 and 11 focus on this first agreement. Second, the agreement for each current session must be established. Numbers 6 through 10 emphasize essentials required here.

ESTABLISHING THE RULES OF ENGAGEMENT

The coach and the client must begin the relationship with clear communication by getting their expectations (and misconceptions) out on the table. The coaching relationship will get off to a good start if the coach sends a welcome packet to the client prior to their first meeting. The packet may include such things as:

- A welcome letter
- A biographical summary and picture of the coach
- A description of what coaching is and is not
- How coaching is similar and different from other helping approaches
- A "Getting to Know You" form for the new client to fill out
- A brief statement on the importance of personal growth
- A blank coaching contract
- Personality or temperament inventories

During their first face-to-face meeting, the rules of engagement must be established, and the coach will need to:

- Determine if this is the best fit for both the coach and the client.
- Explain what coaching is and what it isn't.
- Set the parameters of the coaching relationship.
- Determine the logistics of when, where, and how often you will meet.
- Decide on the frequency and methods of contact outside of regular coaching appointments.
- Determine the overall objective to be achieved by being coached.
- Decide on the key issues to be addressed in the first several sessions.
- Discuss logistical considerations of fees, billing, and methods of payments.
- Agree on policy for a canceled session.

- Explain the rebate policy (if used).
- Clarify who is involved with the coaching relationship, such as a third party or sponsor.
- Discuss confidentiality and other ethical considerations.
- Create a written contract.
- Set dates for several upcoming appointments.

It is well-advised for the coach to have legal counsel review a generic written contract before asking clients to sign it. This can be the shell agreement that the coach completes for each client.

ESTABLISHING AND MAINTAINING AGREEMENTS AT EACH SKILL LEVEL

It is essential that a coaching agreement is reached for each specific coaching conversation. As one of my mentors, Judy Sabah, MCC, declared, "Unless you get a solid coaching agreement, you're doing nothing more than having a friendly conversation!" The ICF has set out specific skills and behaviors expected for establishing and maintaining agreements at each of the three levels of credentials: Associate Certified Coach (ACC), Professional Certified Coach (PCC), and Master Certified Coach (MCC).

MINIMUM SKILL REQUIREMENTS AT THE ASSOCIATE LEVEL

At an ACC level, the minimum standard of skill that must be demonstrated to achieve a passing score for competency 3 is that the coach invites the client to identify what the client wants to accomplish in the session and the coach attends to that agenda throughout the coaching, unless the client indicates otherwise.

KEY SKILLS EVALUATED

1. The clarity and depth in creating an agreement for the session
2. The coach's ability to partner well with the client in the creation of agreement, measures of success, and issues to be addressed
3. The coach's ability to attend to the client's agenda throughout the session

Specifically, ACC applicants are assessed on the following skills within competency 3 as part of the performance evaluation process:

- Coach and client reach an agreement on what the client wants to accomplish in the session.
- Coach invites the client to identify their desired coaching outcome.
- Coach attends to the agenda set by the client throughout the session, unless the client indicates otherwise.
- Coach shows curiosity about the client and how the client relates to what they want to accomplish.

An applicant will not receive a passing score for the Establishes and Maintains Agreements competency on the associate performance evaluation if the coach chooses the topic for the client or if the coach does not coach around the topic the client has chosen.

MINIMUM SKILL REQUIREMENTS AT THE PROFESSIONAL LEVEL

The PCC markers describe minimum skills expected for the Professional Certified Coach. There are four markers for Establishes and Maintains Agreements. Note the emphasis on the coach partnering with the client. The markers are as follows:

1. The coach partners with the client to identify or reconfirm what the client wants to **accomplish** in this session.
2. The coach partners with the client to define or reconfirm **measure(s) of success** for what the client wants to accomplish in this session.
3. The coach inquires about or explores what is **important** or **meaningful** to the client about what they want to accomplish in this session.
4. The coach partners with the client to define what the client believes they need to **address** in order to achieve what they want to accomplish in this session.

The professional coach will explore each of these markers in depth with the client, making sure there is complete understanding of what the client wants to accomplish. At times, several questions may be useful in arriving at a complete understanding. Here are some possible questions for each marker from which the coach may want to choose.

Marker 1: Wants to **accomplish**:

- What's the most important thing you want to work on today?

- What result do you want to take away from our conversation today?
- What would you like to accomplish in our session today?
- What would you like to have at the end of our conversation that you don't have now?
- What would it take to hit a "home run" in our conversation today?
- What would you like to be different for you forty-five minutes from now?

Marker 2: Define **measures of success:**

- How will we measure success in our conversation today?
- How will you know that we have accomplished our goal for today?

Marker 3: What's **important** or **meaningful** about that:

- Help me understand what makes this important to you.
- Of all the topics you could have chosen, what makes this the one you've settled on for today?
- What makes this issue meaningful for you?
- If we can accomplish that, what will that give you?
- What level of urgency do you have around that issue?

Marker 4: Needs to **address:**

- As we talk about all this, what key points should we be sure to cover?
- What aspects are important to consider?

- What various issues need to be addressed?
- What issues need to be resolved as we talk?

The coach must reflect back to the client for confirmation what was heard on each of these markers. If the client's answer on any of them is ambiguous, the coach must explore them further with the client to remove the ambiguity. At times, the client may state information regarding one of the markers before the coach asks questions for that marker. In this case, the coach must acknowledge that information and reflect it back to the client. The coach must be aware of the client's use of words or phrases and clarify their meaning.

These suggested coaching agreement questions should be asked in a conversational manner rather than mechanically, as from a checklist. Marker 1 (*accomplish*) sets the topic and direction for the conversation, as well as establishes specific targets for which to shoot. Marker 2 (*measure*) establishes a specific "bullseye" for the target. Marker 3 (*importance*) provides the coach with a deeper look into the client's values and priorities. Marker 4 (*key points*) sets out the agenda or roadmap for the coach to guide the conversation.

The original 2014 PCC markers contained a fifth marker:

The coach continues the conversation in the direction of the client's **desired outcome**, unless the client indicates otherwise. This marker is covered by descriptive statement 10 (page 76): "Continues coaching in the direction of the client's desired outcome." While this is no longer a marker, continuing in the client's desired direction still is an essential behavior. The experienced coach will check with the client occasionally, perhaps two or three times in a session, to make sure that the conversation is on target and serving the client well.

MINIMUM SKILL REQUIREMENTS AT THE MASTER LEVEL

At an MCC level, the minimum standard of skill that must be demonstrated to achieve a passing score for competency 3 is that the coach fully explores with the client what they want to work on. The coach partners with the client to thoroughly explore the topic of importance to the client, measures of success, and any changes in the direction of the coaching conversation. Through a partnering discussion, the coach ensures that both are clear about the agenda, the measures of success, and the issues to be discussed, and the coach attends to that agenda and those measures throughout the coaching, unless redirected by the client. The coach regularly checks with the client throughout the session to ensure that the client's goals for the session are being achieved and that the direction and process are supporting the client in moving toward their desired outcome.

KEY SKILLS EVALUATED

1. The clarity and depth in creating an agreement for the session
2. The coach's ability to partner well with the client in the creation of agreement, measures of success, and issues to be addressed
3. The coach's ability to attend to the client's agenda throughout the session

Specifically, MCC applicants are assessed on the following skills within the Establishes and Maintains Agreements competency as part of the performance evaluation process:

- Coach partners with the client to explore the topic or focus of the session at a level that is meaningful to the client.
- Coach partners with the client to keep the desired outcome as a guide to the coaching conversation in a flexible, gentle, and natural manner.
- Coach notices subtle shifts in the conversation and invites the client to change direction if the client desires.

A coach will not receive a passing score for the Establishes and Maintains Agreements competency on the MCC performance evaluation if full partnership with the client is not demonstrated. Full partnership will not be demonstrated if the coach chooses the topic(s) for the client or if the coach does not coach around the topic(s) the client has chosen. The evaluation for this competency will also be negatively impacted if the coach does not explore the measures of success for each topic with the client to a degree that achieves clarity about the client's intent or direction for the session, does not allow the client full input into the issues that should be discussed relative to the client's stated objectives for the session, or does not check with the client about whether the client is moving toward what the client wanted from the session.[39]

ASSESSOR QUESTIONS

When listening to a recording for a PCC credential application, assessors are trained to listen for specific behaviors regarding the coaching agreement. The following are some questions an ICF assessor may ask when listening to your recording:

1. Does the coach inquire about the coaching agreement early enough in the session so that they assist in framing the session?
2. Does the coach ask for and receive a topic and goal for the session?
3. Does the coach ask the client to define the session focus?
4. If the client states a topic or goal that is ambiguous, does the coach explore to resolve the ambiguity?
5. Does the coach confirm and articulate back the agreement or focus for the session?
6. Does the coach ask the client to define the desired outcome for the session?
7. Does the coach ask for and receive measures of success for the session?
8. Does the coach explore to resolve the ambiguity if the client's stated measures of success are clearly ambiguous?
9. Does the coach ask what the evidence of success would be for the session?
10. Does the coach reflect back to the client the success measure(s) for the session?
11. Does the coach ask for the meaning or importance of the goal to the client?
12. If the meaning or importance of the goal is evident from what the client said, does the coach acknowledge it?
13. If the client's statement of meaning or importance of the goal is ambiguous, does the coach explore to resolve the ambiguity?
14. Does the coach inquire about the personal and/or professional relevance and/or significance of the client's topic?

15. Does the coach use questions to help the client clarify what achieving the outcome would mean?
16. Does the coach use questions to help the client clarify how motivated s/he is to achieve the goal?
17. Does the coach specifically engage the client in a discussion of what they need to address or resolve in order to achieve the client's stated outcome?
18. If the client volunteers the information, does the coach acknowledge it?
19. Does the coach inquire about what issues would allow for complete achievement of the goal?
20. Does the coach reflect issues back to client that were heard?
21. Does the coach explore what issues must be resolved for the goal to be achieved?
22. If there is no change of direction regarding the client's desired outcome, does the coach continue to help the client move toward that outcome?
23. If there is a change of direction regarding the desired outcome, does the coach obtain the client's consent?
24. If a new and/or competing session goal emerges, does the coach re-contract the coaching session agreement and success measures?[40]

SUMMARY

Establishes and Maintains Agreements means that the coach partners with the client and relevant stakeholders to create clear agreements about the coaching relationship, process, plans, and goals. The coach establishes agreements for the overall coaching engagement, as well as those for each coaching session. Two agreements are required. First, the "rules of engagement" regarding the overall coaching relationship, and second, the agreement for each current session. The four PCC markers delineate what is essential to be covered in this second coaching agreement. Experienced coaches spend significant time thoroughly exploring the presenting issue for each coaching session.

13

Cultivates Trust and Safety

ICF Core Competency 4

*Cultivating trust and safety is the ability to partner
with the client to create a safe, supportive environment that
allows the client to share freely. The coach maintains
a relationship of mutual respect and trust.*

TRUST DOES NOT COME overnight with a new client. Trust comes slowly, bit by bit over time, as it is earned. Here are some ways to deepen trust and develop intimacy with a new client.

In chapter 3 we suggested the coach should . . .

- *Start each session with a 'check-in' time.*
- *Listen deeply, without interrupting.*
- *Honor the client's perspectives, feelings and opinions.*

Trust is a fragile thing and can easily be broken. Avoid these trust-breakers.

Distractions. Many things can take the coach's attention away from the client, including a phone ringing, a text message pinging a cell phone, a person walking by, a baby crying, or a dog barking. When a client sees that the coach no longer is focused on the conversation, the trust level is lowered.

Breaking Confidentiality. In the initial contracting session, the coach pledged that what the client shared would be held in confidence. If the coach shares bits of information about the client with others and that gets back to the client, significant damage is done to the trusting relationship. The client will be reluctant to share anything of significance with the coach from then on.

Lack of Follow-through. When the coach has agreed to do something and fails to do that, the client is less inclined to believe the coach the next time something is promised. Trust levels are diminished.

In order to build trust the coach . . .

- Seeks to understand the client within their context which may include their identity, environment, experiences, values, and beliefs
- Demonstrates respect for the client's identity, perceptions, style, and language and adapts one's coaching to the client
- Acknowledges and respects the client's unique talents, insights, and work in the coaching process
- Shows support, empathy, and concern for the client
- Acknowledges and supports the client's expression of feelings, perceptions, concerns, beliefs and suggestions
- Demonstrates openness and transparency as a way to display vulnerability and build trust with the client[41]

CULTIVATING TRUST AND SAFETY AT EACH SKILL LEVEL

The ICF has set out specific skills and behaviors expected for cultivating trust and safety at each of the three levels of credentials: Associate Certified Coach (ACC), Professional Certified Coach (PCC), and Master Certified Coach (MCC).

MINIMUM SKILL REQUIREMENTS AT THE ASSOCIATE LEVEL

At the ACC level, the coach attends to the client's agenda, but is attached to his or her own performance, and therefore trust and intimacy is not the strongest competency.

KEY SKILLS EVALUATED

1. The coach's depth of connection to and support of the client
2. The coach's demonstration of trust in and respect for the client and the client's processes of thinking, creating
3. The coach's willingness to be open, authentic, and vulnerable with the client to build mutual trust

At an ACC level, the minimum standard of skill that must be demonstrated to receive a passing score for competency 4 is that the coach shows genuine concern, support and respect for the client and is attuned to client's beliefs, perceptions, learning style, and personal being at a basic level.

Specifically, ACC applicants are assessed on the following skills within competency 4 as part of the performance evaluation process:

- Coach acknowledges client insights and learning in the moment.
- Coach explores the client's expression of feelings, perceptions, concerns, beliefs, or suggestions.
- Coach expresses support and concern for the client, which may focus on the client's context, problem, or situation rather than the client holistically.

A coach will not receive a passing score for the Cultivates Trust and Safety competency in the ACC performance evaluation if the coach demonstrates significant interest in the coach's own view of the situation rather than the client's view of the situation; if the coach does not seek information from the client about the client's thinking around the situation, if the coach is unsupportive or disrespectful to the client, or if the coach's attention seems to be on their own performance or demonstration of knowledge about the topic rather than on the client.[42]

MINIMUM SKILL REQUIREMENTS AT THE PROFESSIONAL LEVEL

At the PCC level, the coach may have some degree of trust with the client, and they may have a connected relationship. However, the coach still is conscious of presenting the image of a good coach and is less willing to risk or to not know. This mindset stands in the way of the coach having complete trust and intimacy with himself or herself, with the client, and for the coaching relationship in general.

At the PCC level, the PCC markers are used as guidelines for minimum skills required. These markers are the skills or behaviors that can guide a coach's progress in acquiring skills to cultivate trust and safety as one develops as a coach.

There are four markers for the Cultivating Trust and Safety competency.[43]

1. The coach acknowledges and respects the **client's unique talents, insights,** and **work** in the coaching process.
2. The coach shows **support, empathy,** or **concern** for the client.
3. The coach acknowledges and supports the **client's expression** of feelings, perceptions, concerns, beliefs, or suggestions.
4. The coach partners with the client by inviting the **client to respond** in any way to the coach's contributions and accepts the client's response.

MINIMUM SKILL REQUIREMENTS AT THE MASTER LEVEL

At the MCC level, the coach is keenly aware of a state of deep trust with the client that arises in the moment from in-depth conversations. The coach is comfortable not knowing as one of the best states in which to expand awareness. The coach is willing to be vulnerable with the client and have the client be vulnerable with him or her. The coach is confident in himself or herself, in the process, and in the client as a full partner in the relationship. There is a sense of complete ease and naturalness in conversations, so the coach does not have to work at coaching.

KEY SKILLS EVALUATED

1. The coach's depth of connection to and support of the client
2. The coach's depth of trust in and respect for the client and the client's processes of thinking, creating
3. The coach's willingness to be open, authentic, and vulnerable with the client to build mutual trust

At an MCC level, the minimum standard of skill that must be demonstrated to receive a passing score for competency 4 is that the coach demonstrates complete and open trust in the client and the process by engaging the client as an equal partner in the coaching, and by the coach's willingness to be vulnerable with the client and creating a safe space for the client to be vulnerable in return.

The MCC level coach demonstrates a complete confidence in self, the coaching process, the client as a whole, and a genuine curiosity about and respect for the client's perceptions, learning style, and personal being. The client is treated as an equal partner in the relationship with a full invitation to participate in the development and creation of the coaching process and their own new learning and behaviors.

Specifically, MCC applicants are assessed on the following skills within competency 4 as part of the performance evaluation process:

- Coach engages the client as an equal partner in a collaborative coaching process.
- Coach exhibits genuine curiosity about the client as a whole person by inviting the client to share more about themself or their identity.

- Coach provides space for the client to fully express themself, share feelings, beliefs, and perspectives, without judgment.
- Coach acknowledges the client and celebrates client progress.

A coach will not receive a passing score for the Cultivates Trust and Safety competency on the MCC performance evaluation if the coach does not treat the client as a full partner, choosing not only the agenda but also participating in the creation of the coaching process itself. Lack of full partnership will be demonstrated if the coach exhibits an interest in the coach's view of the situation rather than the client's view, does not seek information from the client about the client's thinking, does not seek information about the client's goals, or the coach demonstrates a lack of interest in or disrespect toward the client as a whole. In addition, the evaluation will be negatively impacted if the coach does not invite the client to share their thinking on an equal level with the coach or if the coach chooses the direction and approach without significant input from the client. Any indication that the coach is teaching rather than coaching will also result in a score below the MCC level for this competency area.[44]

ASSESSOR QUESTIONS

1. Through language, actions, or attitudes, does the coach create a safe space for the client to explore and work?
2. Does the friendly exchange of language between the coach and the client provide evidence that they have a comfortable, trusting relationship?

3. Does the coach use specific affirming language, such as, "Seems like you've done some good thinking around this"?

4. Does the coach continually seek the client's opinion throughout the session?

5. Does the coach relate to the client through eye contact?

6. Does the coach seek to identify with the client through such things as matching the client's vocal rhythms, mirroring the client's body language, or incorporating verbal expressions?

7. Does the coach recognize and respect the client's self-concept and identity (the who)?

8. Does the coach recognize and affirm the client's courage and willingness to change?

9. Does the coach recognize and acknowledge behavioral challenges faced by or behavioral changes made by client?

10. Does the coach incorporate some of the client's life or work history or personal growth into the conversation?

11. Does the coach refrain from communicating anything negative about the client, whether through words, body language, or tone of voice?

12. Does the coach let the client set the pace and appropriately match the client's pace, rhythm, and energy levels?

13. Does the coach ask specifically, "Tell me how I can support you here"?

14. Does the coach make empathic comments; express confidence in the client's capabilities; reflect the client's progress; or acknowledge successes, strengths, and unique characteristics?

15. Does the coach demonstrate patience during the client's processing?

16. Does the coach use specific language, such as, "Tell me more about your thinking around this"?
17. Does the coach maintain silence until the client is done speaking?
18. Does the coach use silence that allows the client to process thinking and feeling?
19. Does the coach invite the client to disagree with the coach?
20. Does the coach affirmatively encourage the client to continue to express herself or himself?[45]

SUMMARY

Cultivating trust and safety is the ability to partner with the client to create a safe, supportive environment that allows the client to share freely, while maintaining a relationship of mutual respect and trust. Trust and safety form the foundation for an effective coaching relationship. Without it, the coaching will produce no positive results. The essence of this competency is in creating a safe space for the client to do the work. Genuine caring, authentic respect, and deep listening help to quickly establish a trusting relationship.

14

Maintains Presence

ICF Core Competency 5

*The coach is fully conscious and present
with the client, employing a style that is open, flexible,
grounded and confident.*

COACHING WELL DEMANDS FOCUS and concentration. It requires engaging the client with your whole being – intellectually, emotionally, physically and spiritually – for the entire conversation. The coach who maintains presence . . .

- Remains focused, observant, empathetic and responsive to the client.
- Demonstrates curiosity during the coaching process.
- Manages one's emotions to stay present with the client.
- Demonstrates confidence in working with strong client emotions during the coaching process.
- Is comfortable working in a space of not knowing.
- Creates or allows space for silence, pause, or reflection.[46]

COACHING PRESENCE AT EACH SKILL LEVEL

The ICF has set out specific skills and behaviors expected for coaching presence at each of the three levels of credentials: Associate Certified Coach (ACC), Professional Certified Coach (PCC), and Master Certified Coach (MCC).

MINIMUM SKILL REQUIREMENTS AT THE ASSOCIATE LEVEL

At the ACC level, the coach attends to the client's agenda, but is attached to his or her own performance and therefore presence is diluted by the coach's own attention to self. Much of the time the coach substitutes thinking and analysis for presence and responsiveness.

KEY SKILLS EVALUATED

1. The coach's depth of focus on and partnership with the client
2. The coach's depth of observation and use of the whole of the client in the coaching process
3. The coach's ability to create space for reflection and remain present to the client through both conversation and silence

At an ACC level, the minimum standard of skill that must be demonstrated to receive a passing score for competency 5 is that the coach demonstrates curiosity about the client and the client's agenda and is responsive to the information the client offers throughout the session.

Specifically, ACC applicants are assessed on the following skills within competency 5 as part of the performance evaluation process:

- Coach is curious throughout the session.
- Coach acknowledges situations that the client presents.
- Coach allows the client to direct the conversation at least some of the time.

The ICF notes that the skills to cultivate trust and safety and maintain presence are quite related. Therefore, a coach will not receive a passing score for the Maintains Presence competency on the ACC performance evaluation if the coach demonstrates significant interest in the coach's own view of the situation rather than exploring the client's view of the situation, does not seek information from the client about the client's thinking around the situation or is unresponsive to that information, the coach consistently directs the conversation, or the attention seems to be on the coach's own performance or demonstration of knowledge about the topic.[47]

MINIMUM SKILL REQUIREMENTS AT THE PROFESSIONAL LEVEL

At the PCC level, the coach attends to the client's agenda, but drives the coaching conversation and choice of tools. The coach chooses either an objective or a subjective perspective, but rarely holds both simultaneously. The coach tends toward problem-solving, versus simply being in the moment with the client. The coach chooses ways to move, versus letting the client teach the coach possible ways to move. Partnership with the client is evident, but mixed, with the coach as the expert and greater than the client. The coach may be aware of whether and how much value they are adding to the client.

At the PCC level, the PCC markers are used as guidelines for minimum skills required. These markers are the skills or behaviors that can guide a coach's progress in acquiring creating awareness skills as one develops as a coach. There are five markers for the Coaching Presence competency.[48]

1. Coach acts in response to the **whole person** of the client (the **who**).
2. Coach acts in response to what the client wants to **accomplish** throughout this session (the **what**).
3. Coach partners with the client by supporting the client to **choose what happens** in this session.
4. Coach demonstrates **curiosity** to learn more about the client.
5. Coach allows for **silence**, pause, or reflection.

MINIMUM SKILL REQUIREMENTS AT THE MASTER LEVEL

At the MCC level, the coach is a completely connected observer of the client. The connection is to the whole of who the client is, how the client learns, and what the client has to teach the coach. The coach is ready to be touched by the client and welcomes signals that create resonance for both the coach and client. The coach evidences a complete curiosity that is undiluted by a need to perform. The coach is in fully partnered conversation with client. The coach trusts that value is inherent in the process versus needing to create value.

KEY SKILLS EVALUATED

1. The coach's depth of focus on and partnership with the client
2. The coach's depth of observation and use of the whole of the client in the coaching process
3. The coach's ability to create space for reflection and remain present to the client through both conversation and silence

At an MCC level, the minimum standard of skill that must be demonstrated to receive a passing score for competency 5 is that the coach is fully partnering with the client in the coaching dialogue and is a connected observer to the client, holding both objective and emotional perspectives simultaneously. The connection is to the whole of the client, who the client is, what the client wants, how the client learns and creates, and how the client leads the coaching conversation. The coach evidences a genuine curiosity in the client. As with the Cultivates Trust and Safety competency, the coach is in a complete partnership with the client where the client is an equal or greater contributor to the conversation and direction of the coaching than the coach. At the MCC level, the conversation between coach and client is equal and easy, even in uncomfortable moments.

Specifically, MCC applicants are assessed on the following skills within competency 5 as part of the performance evaluation process:

*   Coach responds to the client in a manner that keeps the conversation flowing with the client leading the way.

- Coach remains curious and attentive to the client, exploring what the client needs throughout the session.
- Coach engages in the coaching conversation with ease and fluidity.
- Coach leverages silence to support the client and the client's growth.

A coach will not receive a passing score for competency 5 on the MCC performance evaluation if the coach does not treat the client as a full partner, choosing not only the agenda but also participating in the creation of the coaching process itself. Such lack of full partnership is demonstrated if the coach exhibits interest in the coach's view of the situation rather than the client's view, does not seek information from the client about the client's thinking, does not seek information about the client's goals, or if the coach's attention seems to be on the coach's own performance or demonstration of knowledge. In addition, the evaluation will be negatively impacted if the coach does not invite the client to share their thinking on an equal level with the coach.[49]

BEING 100% PRESENT

The essence of this competency is to be 100% present, which has some obvious implications.

Things you must do:

- Be well rested. Coaching takes both emotional and physical energy.
- Remove distractions.
- Review notes from the previous coaching session.
- Be prepared. Get centered and focused.

- Discipline your mind to give full attention to the client.
- Listen actively.
- Stick with the client's agenda.
- Tune into the client's emotions.
- Participate with, rather than lead the client.
- Be flexible.
- Let go of your own solutions.
- "Dance in the moment," realizing that in this dance it is the client who leads, while the coach follows.
- Ask questions from various angles to help the client gain perspective.
- Let go of that brilliant comment you were about to make when the client moved on.
- Remain curious. Let your questions arise out of curiosity.
- Trust your instinct and ask that risky question.

Things you don't do:

- Check e-mail or text messages.
- Answer the phone.
- Daydream or let your mind wander.
- Plan the day's to-do list.

COACH THE PERSON, NOT THE PROBLEM!

PCC Marker 1 says, "The coach acts in response to the **whole person** of the client (the who)." Perhaps you have heard the often-repeated phrase, "Coach the person, not the problem." What does this mean?

As a coach, my aim is to inspire clients to grow both personally and professionally, as well as to assist them in dealing with their presenting issues in a coaching session. I want them to expand awareness about themselves, as well as gain insight into their situation.

In the coaching world, we have developed certain words with specialized meanings. These include the words *who* and *what*. There are *what* questions and then there are *who* questions. What's the difference?

To clarify, the words *who* and *what* have nothing to do with starting a question with that word. Rather, they are categories of types of questions. *Who* questions focus on the client's personhood or being or inner life. *What* questions focus on the client's actions or doing or outer life. Both kind of questions questions are essential in coaching.

Many presenting issues surfaced by a client when establishing the agreement are *what* issues. These have to do with issues such as setting goals, taking necessary steps to achieve a goal, or solving a pressing problem. Successfully dealing with the presenting issue in a coaching conversation is essential in serving the client well. *What* questions typically assist a client in thinking through issues that require action. Examples:

- With whom do you need to speak to resolve that issue?
- How could you arrive at a solution to this problem?
- What would doing that accomplish?

At the same time, an even higher priority in serving the client well is stimulating growth in the client as a person. *What* questions are less effective in promoting personal growth. Instead, *who* questions can invite deeper reflection and are more likely to lead to growth as a person and as a leader. Stated another way, our goal in coaching is first to serve clients by focusing on the presenting issue or problem that they want to resolve. However, a second and greater objective is to stimulate growth and transformation in them as persons and as leaders. This is accomplished by asking more *who* questions that focus on personhood and being. Examples:

- How does that relate to your personal core values?
- In what ways would that decision impact your marriage and family?
- Since you see yourself as a person of integrity and character, what impact would that decision have on your self-image?

Here is a key to coaching the person, not just the problem. Inquire as to how the presenting issue impacts other areas of the client's life. Think of the things that comprise a person's inner life—priorities; core values; emotions; self-image; hopes and dreams; past mistakes and regrets; relationships of various kinds, including marriage, family, extended family, coworkers, neighbors, and friends; spirituality; health and physical well-being; worldview; and so forth. Ask powerful *who* questions that invite the client to consider how the presenting issue impacts these various areas. Or do it the opposite way. Ask how a certain area regarding their inner life influences the presenting issue. Either way, in using this approach a coach combines focusing on the presenting issue, plus using *who* questions that invite deeper reflection and stimulate transformation and personal growth.

Coach the whole person, not just the problem!

ASSESSOR QUESTIONS

1. Does the coach focus just on the client's topic or problem, or does the coach focus on the whole person, including such things as when or how the client,

thinks, creates, relates, learns, feels, values, views his or her world, and chooses to be in the world?

2. Is the coach generally observant, empathetic, and responsive?

3. Does the coach treat the client's emotions respectfully, responsibly, and with unconditional positive regard?

4. If there is a distinct energy shift, does the coach notice and inquire about the shift?

5. Does the coach share observational feedback with the client when the client's vocal, verbal, or body rhythms change?

6. Does the coach demonstrate curiosity with the intent of learning more?

7. Does the coach genuinely and authentically inquire about the client's agenda?

8. Does the coach genuinely and authentically inquire about aspects of the client as a person?

9. Does the coach regularly seek the client's input about ideas and concepts?

10. Does the coach extend an invitation to codesign or cocreate the session focus and direction?

11. Does the coach check in on the focus and direction of the conversation during the session?

12. Does the coach avoid staying just in his or her own frame of reference?

13. Does the coach invite disagreement from the client?

14. If offering opinions, does the coach partner with the client by extending an invitation for the client to use, or not use, the opinion as the client sees fit?

15. Does the coach hear and respect the client's frame of reference and thinking and, as appropriate, share his or her own thinking and frame of reference without attachment?

16. Does the coach hold and honor the client's opposing viewpoints?
17. Does the coach recognize and reflect when, where and with whom the client's choices exist?
18. Does the coach clarify his or her own understanding of the choices the client has?
19. Does the coach inquire about and champion the client's capability to assess his or her own learning?
20. Does the coach inquire about the client's sense of being, the client's situation and the client's actions?[50]

SUMMARY

Maintains Presence is the ability to be fully conscious and create spontaneous relationship with the client, employing a style that is open, flexible, and confident. Coaching presence focuses on the coach's ability to be 100% present with the client. Coaching presence is very broad, in that it encompasses every aspect of each coaching conversation. It requires intense focus and concentration, as well as flexibility and the ability to "dance" in the moment with the client.

15

Listens Actively

ICF Core Competency 6

Listens Actively is the ability to focus on what the client is and is not saying, to fully understand what is being communicated in the context of the client systems and to support client self-expression.

LISTENING ACTIVELY IS NOT a passive endeavor but requires intense focus. The good listener is focused completely on what the person is saying and processes their sharing in a reflective comprehensive way. The listener takes in the person's ideas and replies constructively.

ACTIVE LISTENING AT EACH SKILL LEVEL

The ICF has set out specific skills and behaviors expected for active listening at each of the three levels of credentials: Associate Certified Coach (ACC), Professional Certified Coach (PCC), and Master Certified Coach (MCC).

MINIMUM SKILL REQUIREMENTS AT THE ASSOCIATE LEVEL

At the ACC level, the coach hears what the client says and responds to it, but only at an obvious surface level. Often the coach is fixated on answering the questions *What's the problem? How do I help fix it?* and *How do I give value in fixing it?*

At the ACC level to listen actively, the coach[51]

1. Considers the client's context, identity, environment, experiences, values, and beliefs to enhance understanding of what the client is communicating.
2. Reflects or summarizes what the client communicated to ensure clarity and understanding.
3. Recognizes and inquires when there is more to what the client is communicating.
4. Notices, acknowledges, and explores the client's emotions, energy shifts, non-verbal cues or other behaviors.
5. Integrates the client's words, tone of voice, and body language to determine the full meaning of what is being communicated.
6. Notices trends in the client's behaviors and emotions across sessions to discern themes and patterns.

KEY SKILLS EVALUATED

1. The coach's depth of attention to what the client communicates in relation to the client and the client's agenda

2. The coach's ability to hear on multiple levels including both the emotional and substantive content of the words

3. The coach's ability to hear underlying beliefs, thinking, creating, and learning that are occurring for the client including recognizing incongruities in language, emotions, and actions

4. The coach's ability to hear and integrate the client's language and to invite the client to deeper exploration

At an ACC level, the minimum standard of skill that must be demonstrated to receive a passing score for competency 6 is that the coach listens to what the client communicates in relation to the client's agenda, responds to what the client offers to ensure clarity of understanding, and integrates what the client has communicated to support the client in achieving their agenda. The coach's behaviors in this competency may include listening to what the client has communicated verbally, as well as what the client may communicate in other ways, such as tone of voice, energy or emotional shifts, or body language.

Specifically, ACC applicants are assessed on the following skills within competency 6 as part of the performance evaluation process:

- Coach uses summarizing or paraphrasing to make sure they understood the client correctly.
- Coach makes observations that support the client in creating new associations.
- Coach co-creates a shared vision with the client.

A coach will not receive a passing score for the Listens Actively competency on the ACC performance evaluation if the coach does not demonstrate listening that is focused on and responding to what the client communicates or the coach's responses are not related to what the client is trying to achieve. The coach will not receive a passing grade on the ACC performance evaluation if the coach appears to be listening for the place where the coach can demonstrate their knowledge about the topic or tell the client what to do about the topic.[52]

MINIMUM SKILL REQUIREMENTS AT THE PROFESSIONAL LEVEL

At the PCC level, the coach is listening on a very conscious level. The listening is focused on the client's agenda and can change direction if the client changes direction. The direction change may or may not be best for the topic at hand. The coach is focused on what the client is saying, but more from the perspective of gathering information that fits into the coach's particular tool or discovery model. Listening tends to be more linear and concentrates on the content of words. The coach is listening for answers, thinking of the next question to ask, or looking for what to do with what is heard. The coach tries to fit what is heard into the best model. The coach often will respond out of that model rather than from the client's model. Listening includes some depth but often misses key nuances that a master level coach would catch. Listening tends to be session by session versus cumulative.

At the PCC level, the PCC markers are used as guidelines for minimum skills required. These markers are skills or behaviors that can guide a coach's progress in acquiring creating awareness skills as one develops as a coach. There are seven markers for the Listens Actively competency.[53]

1. Coach's questions and observations are **customized** by using what the coach has learned about who the client is or the client's situation.
2. Coach inquires about or explores the **words** the client uses.
3. Coach inquires about or explores the client's **emotions**.
4. Coach explores the client's **energy shifts**, nonverbal cues or other behaviors.
5. Coach inquires about or explores how the client currently **perceives themself** or their world.
6. Coach allows the client to complete speaking **without interrupting** unless there is a stated coaching purpose to do so.
7. Coach succinctly **reflects** or **summarizes** what the client communicated to ensure the client's clarity and understanding.

MINIMUM SKILL REQUIREMENTS AT THE MASTER LEVEL

At the MCC level, the coach's listening is completely attuned as a learner. Listening happens at the logical, emotional, and organic level at the same time. The listening is both linear and non-linear, and responses from the coach evidence learning about the client at many levels. The coach recognizes both one's own and the client's ability of intuitive and energetic perception that is felt when the client speaks of important things, when new growth is occurring for the client, and when the client is finding a more powerful sense of self. The coach's listening is in the present, but the coach also hears the client's future being envisioned. The coach hears the totality of the client's greatness and gifts, as well as limiting beliefs and patterns. The coach's listening is cumulative from session to session, as well as throughout each individual session.

Here are six statements describing active listening at the MCC level.[54]

The coach . . .

1. Considers the client's context, identity, environment, experiences, values, and beliefs to enhance understanding of what the client is communicating
2. Reflects or summarizes what the client communicated to ensure clarity and understanding
3. Recognizes and inquires when there is more to what the client is communicating
4. Notices, acknowledges, and explores the client's emotions, energy shifts, non-verbal cues, or other behaviors
5. Integrates the client's words, tone of voice and body language to determine the full meaning of what is being communicated
6. Notices trends in the client's behaviors and emotions across sessions to discern themes and patterns

KEY SKILLS EVALUATED

1. The coach's depth of attention to what the client communicates in relation to the client and the client's agenda
2. The coach's ability to hear on multiple levels, including both the emotional and substantive content of the words
3. The coach's ability to hear underlying beliefs, thinking, creating, and learning that are occurring for the client

including recognizing incongruities in language, emotions, and actions

4. The coach's ability to hear and integrate the client's language and to invite the client to deeper exploration.

At an MCC level, the minimum standard of skill that must be demonstrated to receive a passing score for competency 6 is that the coach listens as a learner and demonstrates an ability to listen at the logical and emotional level at the same time. Responses from the coach evidence learning about the client at multiple levels. The coach's responses evidence that the coach is hearing the client's intuitive abilities, the client's energy, when the client speaks of important things, when new growth is occurring for the client, how that growth is related to the client's stated objectives and agenda, and when the client is finding, creating, and using a more powerful sense of self. The coach is also able to hear the client's current thinking and growth and relate it to the future the client is trying to create. An MCC level coach hears the totality of the client's greatness and gifts as well as limiting beliefs and patterns. The coach's listening is cumulative from session to session and throughout each individual session.

Specifically, MCC applicants are assessed on the following skills within competency 6:

- Coach responds to client with an invitation into a deeper exploration of client thinking and behaviors
- Coach's responses to the client demonstrates an understanding of the client's emotions, energy, or learning and growth, in alignment with the client's agenda
- Coach reflects what the client communicates in relation to the context of the whole person

A coach will not receive a passing score for the Listens Actively competency on the MCC performance evaluation if the coach does not demonstrate listening that is based on the whole client and an ability to hear the client's thinking, learning, and feeling at multiple levels. The coach will not receive a passing grade at this level if the listening is filtered only through the coach's methods of thinking, learning, and creating and does not actively hear and use as a significant coaching tool, the client's methods of thinking, learning, and creating. The score for this competency will also be negatively impacted if nuances of the client's language are not reflected in the coach's responses, or if the coach does not respond to what the client communicates, the coach's response is not related to what the client is trying to achieve, or the coach's listening is primarily focused on the client's problems or weaknesses. The coach will not receive a passing grade on the MCC performance evaluation if the coach appears to be listening for the place where the coach can demonstrate their knowledge about the topic or tell the client what to do about the topic.[55]

REALITIES ABOUT LISTENING

- Listening is a foundational coaching skill.
- Listening can be a rare gift to others. (Estimates indicate less than 5% of people feel truly heard.)
- Listening is hard to do well.
- Listening well is a critical skill and is essential to good coaching.
- There is no point in asking powerful questions if you are not going to listen deeply.
- Effective coaches observe the 80/20 rule (listen 80% of the time; talk 20% of the time).

- *Listen* and *silent* are spelled with the same letters. (Let silence do the heavy listening!)

Listening is *not* passive, but requires actively, intentionally, and intuitively grasping facts, feelings, mindsets, etc., of what is *and* is not said.

LISTENING ACTIVELY MEANS . . .

- Listening without an agenda
- Distinguishing between the words, the tone of voice, and body language
- Understanding the essence of the client's communication
- Helping the client gain clarity and perspective, rather than being engaged in the story
- Being curious and interested
- Quieting your mind
- Creating a safe space for another person
- Exploring possibilities (*not* giving answers)
- Reflecting back
- Really *getting* the other person

LISTENING TOOLS FOR YOUR LISTENING TOOLBOX

The more listening tools you have available, the better equipped you will be for effective listening. Let's examine non-listening habits and then look at beginning, intermediate, advanced, and masterful listening skills.

NON-LISTENING HABITS

There are both passive non-listening and active non-listening.

- Passive non-listening is *daydreaming* where your mind is a million miles away. Suddenly you realize that you have not heard a word the person has been saying for the past bit of time.
- Active non-listening often involves hearing the words but focusing on planning your response. Here are some examples of active non-listening:
  - *Internal Listening* – You are hearing what is being said, but your focus is on your own intellectual and emotional reactions to what is being said. (If your listening prompts you to want to tell your own story, you're doing internal listening! This is known as 'conversational narcissism' – a desire to take over a conversation, to do most of the talking and to turn the focus on yourself.[56])
  - *Argumentative Listening* – You are listening only to defeat the other person's points or arguments.
  - *Therapeutic Listening* – You are listening to analyze what's wrong with them and how to fix them.

BEGINNING LISTENING

Keep in mind that effective listening calls for more than just silence. Some kind of response is needed to demonstrate to the person that you are listening, as well as providing the person the chance to confirm that you are hearing accurately or to correct what is being heard, if slightly off. There are five beginning listening skills:

- *Posture* – Your posture should be open rather than closed (such as crossing your arms or legs in a way that blocks them out). Some like to mirror the other person's posture as a subtle way of empathizing.

- *Silence* – Not saying anything but communicating your interest by good eye contact and facial expressions.
- *Grunts or para-verbals* – Non-committal sounds that indicate you are listening (such as hmm, uh-huh, oh, yeah, mmm)
- *Door-Openers* – Words that invite the person to keep talking (*say more, tell me more, fascinating, really, wow, no kidding, interesting*)
- *Parroting* – Repeating key words or phrases the person has just said. (This has the effect of inviting the person to talk more about that.)

INTERMEDIATE LISTENING

There are two intermediate listening skills:

- *Summarizing* – You take the content of several sentences the person has said and condense it into a short sentence.
- *Paraphrasing* – Similar to summarizing, this is when you take the content of several sentences, process it in your mind, and state it back to them in a shortened form, using your own words.

ADVANCED LISTENING

There are two advanced listening skills:

- *Empathetic Listening* – You paraphrase the content, plus you mention the feelings or emotions that you have observed. In empathetic listening you are mirroring back both the content and their perceived feelings. The feelings must be stated tentatively since it is challenging to be 100% accurate. Feelings are most often picked up through facial expressions, body language, tone of voice or choice of words. Empathetic listening should not be overdone.

- *360 Degree Listening* (or *Global Listening*) – This is when you listen intently to:
  o What the other person is saying, picking up both content and feelings
  o Your own intuition, inner knowing, or gut reactions
  o Whispers of the Holy Spirit (or your higher power)

  Impressions from the latter two must be stated conditionally rather than as factual since you may not be completely accurate in what you are picking up.

In a conversation with a friend who had buried his wife just one week earlier, I observed that he was putting on a brave face, indicating that everything was all right. Suddenly the thought came to me, "He's contemplating suicide." At a break in the conversation, I said, "John (not his real name), I'm wondering how much thoughts of harming yourself might be troubling you, if at all?" Tears welled up in his eyes, and he said, "How did you know? That's all I've been thinking about lately."

MASTERFUL LISTENING

Masterful listening is using all of the above listening tools plus listening on multiple levels. There are hundreds of things to listen for. Masterful coaches listen, at best, to only eight to ten things at any given point. Here are some things to consider.

Listen for:

- The content of their words (only 7% of communication is verbal—the actual words they say)
- Words or phrases that have special meaning (Stop and explore these.)
- Frequently used words
- What is *not* being said
- Feelings and emotions
- Tone of voice and inflection
- Changes in pace of speech
- Changes in volume
- Changes in energy level
- Passion and energy
- Strengths, skills, and capabilities
- Frustrations and needs
- Guilt and obligations
- Challenges and barriers
- False assumptions
- Self-limiting beliefs
- Mindset and attitudes
- Values
- Motivations
- Hopes and dreams
- Habits and behavioral patterns
- Facial expressions
- Body language
- Your own intuition

Effective listening involves both listening and giving feedback to determine how accurately you heard the message and feelings the person intended to convey. Feedback can include the listening tools described above. It can also include:

- Clarifying questions (asking the person to explain their intent)
- Unpacking (listing issues)
- Observing ("What I see is . . .")
- Confronting (when the message does not match their perceived feelings)

INSIGHTS FROM RESEARCH

Jack Zenger, CEO, and Joseph Folkman, president of Zenger/ Folkman, a leadership development consultancy, conducted a research study of 3,492 participants in a development program designed to help managers become better coaches. They came to four surprising conclusions about listening skills:[57]

1. Good listening is much more than being silent while the other person talks.
2. Good listening included interactions that build a person's self-esteem.
3. Good listening was seen as a cooperative conversation.
4. Good listeners tended to make suggestions.

Zenger and Folkman suggest six levels of listening:

Level 1 – Create a safe environment where difficult, complex, or emotional issues can be discussed.
Level 2 – Clear away distractions.
Level 3 – Understand the substance of what is said by capturing ideas, asking questions, and restating issues to confirm correct understanding.
Level 4 – Observe non-verbal cues, such as facial expressions, perspiration, respiration rates, gestures, posture, and subtle body-language signals.

Level 5 – Understand, identify, and acknowledge emotions and feelings, and validate these in a supportive, nonjudgmental way.

Level 6 – Ask questions that clarify assumptions held by the other, and help them to see the issue in a new light.

WHAT KEEPS YOU FROM LISTENING WELL?

Listening challenges:

- Mind chatter
- Thinking about what to say next
- Letting go of a brilliant comment that you didn't get to say
- Discomfort with silence
- Multi-tasking
- Trying to fix the other person, instead of just listening

LISTENING TAKES PRACTICE

How do you learn to listen well? Only through practice. It takes repetitive practicing to learn any skill in life, and it takes a great amount of practicing to learn to listen at a deep level.

ASSESSOR QUESTIONS

1. Does the coach listen to how the client processes?
2. Does the coach inquire about specific meaning of the client's language and concepts?
3. Does the coach use what the client has said to form questions, not only about the situation but also about the client's being?

4. Does the coach incorporate the client's actual words into his or her paraphrasing, summarizing, or questioning?

5. Does the coach ask about or reflect the client's emotions by recognizing mood, tone, affect, images, or values?

6. If there is a distinct change in the client's tone, pace, and/or inflection, does the coach notice and inquire about the change?

7. Does the coach share observational feedback when the client's vocal intonation or verbal pacing changes?

8. Does the coach ask about the client's actions or reactions or responses to people, places, or events?

9. Does the coach ask about, identify, or test the client's beliefs, assumptions, values, and perspectives?

10. When listening to a response, does the coach give sufficient time for the client to answer?[58]

SUMMARY

Listening actively is the ability to focus completely on what the client is saying and is not saying, to understand the meaning of what is said in the context of the client's desires, and to support the client's self-expression. Listening is perhaps *the* foundational tool in a coach's toolbox, so coaches must learn to listen at a deep level.

16

Evokes Awareness

ICF Core Competency 7

The coach facilitates client insight and learning
by using tools and techniques such as powerful questioning,
silence, metaphor, or analogy.

THE ICF BELIEVES THAT coaching is all about bringing transformation in clients. Arriving at new insights and perspectives contributes greatly to growth in our clients. Evokes Awareness is one of the most important competencies because it contributes significantly to personal transformation. Evokes Awareness is partly a reworking of the Creating Awareness competency. However, the Evokes Awareness competency also incorporates much of the Powerful Questioning and Direct Communication competencies. As such, it is a significantly expanded competency.

When evoking awareness the coach . . .

1. Considers client experience when deciding what might be most useful.
2. Challenges the client as a way to evoke awareness or insight.

3. Asks questions about the client, such as their way of thinking, values, needs, wants, and beliefs.

4. Asks questions that help the client explore beyond current thinking.

5. Invites the client to share more about their experience in the moment.

6. Notices what is working to enhance client progress.

7. Adjusts the coaching approach in response to the client's needs.

8. Helps the client identify factors that influence current and future patterns of behavior, thinking, or emotion.

9. Invites the client to generate ideas about how they can move forward and what they are willing or able to do.

10. Supports the client in reframing perspectives.

11. Shares observations, insights, and feelings, without attachment, that have the potential to create new learning for the client.[59]

EVOKES AWARENESS AT EACH SKILL LEVEL

The ICF has set out specific skills and behaviors expected for Evokes Awareness at each of the three levels of credentials: Associate Certified Coach (ACC), Professional Certified Coach (PCC), and Master Certified Coach (MCC).

MINIMUM SKILL REQUIREMENTS AT THE ASSOCIATE LEVEL

For the ACC coach, awareness is generated at the level of what will solve the problem or achieve the goal. Awareness is limited generally to that of new techniques, rather than new learning about self.

KEY SKILLS EVALUATED

1. The coach's use of inquiry, exploration, silence, and other techniques that support the client in achieving new or deeper learning and awareness
2. The coach's ability to explore with and evoke exploration by the client of the emotional and substantive meaning of the client's words
3. The coach's ability to explore with and evoke exploration by the client of the underlying beliefs and means of thinking, creating, and learning that are occurring for the client
4. The coach's ability to support the client in exploring new or expanded perspectives or ways of thinking
5. The coach's invitation to and integration of the client's intuition, thinking, and language as critical tools in the coaching process

At an ACC level, the minimum standard of skill that must be demonstrated to receive a passing score for competency 7 is that the coach uses inquiry, exploration, silence, and other techniques to support the client in achieving new or deeper learning and awareness.

Specifically, ACC applicants are assessed on the following skills within competency 7 as part of the performance evaluation process:

- Coach inquires about or explores the client's ideas, beliefs, thinking, emotions, and behaviors in relation to the desired outcome.
- Coach supports the client in viewing the situation from new or different perspectives.

- Coach acknowledges the client's new awareness, learning, and movement toward the desired outcome.

A coach will not receive a passing score for the Evokes Awareness competency on the ACC performance evaluation if the coach focuses consistently on instructing the client or sharing the coach's own knowledge, ideas or beliefs; if the majority of the coach's questions are leading or contain pre-determined answers by the coach, or if the coach's questions and explorations attend to an agenda or issues not set by the client but by the coach.[60]

MINIMUM SKILL REQUIREMENTS AT THE PROFESSIONAL LEVEL

At the PCC level, the coach helps the client to create new awareness by engaging in problem-solving. The majority of awareness is geared to new techniques, while new awareness about the client's being is more limited. Thus, awareness is limited in scope. The coach typically helps the client become aware of particular situations, rather than broadening that learning to all of life.

For the PCC level, the PCC markers are used as guidelines for minimum skills required. These markers are the skills or behaviors that can guide a coach's progress in acquiring creating awareness skills as one develops as a coach. There are eight markers for the Evokes Awareness competency.

1. Coach asks questions **about the client**, such as their current way of thinking, feeling, values, needs, wants, beliefs or behavior.
2. Coach asks questions to help the client explore beyond the client's current thinking or feeling to new or

expanded ways of thinking or feeling about **themself** (the who).

3. Coach asks questions to help the client explore beyond the client's current thinking or feeling to new or expanded ways of thinking or feeling about their **situation** (the what).

4. Coach asks questions to help the client explore beyond current thinking, feeling, or behaving toward the **outcome** the client desires.

5. Coach **shares**—with no attachment—observations, intuitions, comments, thoughts, or feelings, and invites the client's exploration through verbal or tonal invitation.

6. Coach asks clear, direct, primarily **open-ended questions**, one at a time, at a pace that allows for thinking, feeling or reflection by the client.

7. Coach uses language that is generally **clear and concise**.

8. Coach allows the **client** to do most of the talking.[61]

MINIMUM SKILL REQUIREMENTS AT THE MASTER LEVEL

At the MCC level, the coach's invitation to broadly explore an issue significantly outweighs the invitation to solve a specific problem. The coach is as much an explorer as the client. The coach has not concluded what awareness should be, and the coach is willing not to know all the issues. The client's greatness is invited and welcomed. There is no evidence of "fixing" a problem or the client. The coach encourages the client to make the coach aware. The client's voice is more prevalent than the coach's voice. There is a lovely sense of harmony between who the client is and what the client wants. Sharing is done freely back and forth between coach and client. The coach does not force awareness.

KEY SKILLS EVALUATED

1. The coach's use of inquiry, exploration, silence, and other techniques that support the client in achieving new or deeper learning and awareness
2. The coach's ability to explore with and evoke exploration by the client of the emotional and substantive content of the words
3. The coach's ability to explore with and evoke exploration by the client of the underlying beliefs and means of thinking, creating, and learning that are occurring for the client
4. The coach's ability to support the client in exploring new or expanded perspectives or ways of thinking
5. The coach's invitation to and integration of the client's intuition, thinking, and language as critical tools in the coaching process

At an MCC level, the minimum standard of skill that must be demonstrated to receive a passing score for competency 7 is that the coach's invitation to the exploration of important issues precedes and is significantly greater than the invitation to a solution. At an MCC level, the coach's way of being is consistently curious; the coach is willing to not know but allow the exploration to evolve based on the client's thinking, learning, and creating. The coach asks mostly, if not always, direct, evocative questions that are fully responsive to the client in the moment, to the client's agenda and stated objectives, and that require significant thought by the client or take the client to a new place of thinking. The coach makes frequent and full use of the client's language and learning style to craft questions, insights, or observations that provide a space for a client to use and expand their own style of thinking, learning, and creating, and to discover their power, gifts, and strengths. The coach provides sufficient space and encouragement to allow the client to integrate and use new awareness to identify patterns of thinking or behavior, resolve current challenges, achieve current goals, and think how the new awareness may be used in the future.

Specifically, MCC applicants are assessed on the following skills within competency 7 as part of the performance evaluation process:

- Coach partners with the client to explore the client's stories, metaphors and imagery that support growth and learning.
- Coach stimulates new client insights with minimal, precise questions.
- Coach asks questions that challenge the client to explore more deeply or to go beyond current thinking and feeling.
- Coach shares with fluidity insights, observations, or questions from the client's words and actions to foster awareness.

A coach will not receive a passing score for the Evokes Awareness competency on the MCC performance evaluation if the coach does not demonstrate an ability to use questions, insights, silence, or other techniques that encourage the client to deepen their thinking in a larger, more reflective space related to the client or the client's agenda. The evaluation will be negatively impacted if the coach frequently asks questions that keep the client in the past or present when dealing with a situation rather than being forward thinking, or if the coach drives the client toward solutions without fully exploring issues that may be important to gaining a complete solution or accomplishment for the client. The evaluation will also be negatively impacted if the dialogue does not provide sufficient space for the client's full participation in creating awareness; if the coach's communication reflects an agenda or directing of any kind; if the coach does not evidence frequent use of the client's language, learning, thinking, and creating styles; or if the coach does not often create an easy place for the client to engage in deeper thinking, learning, and discovery. The coach will not receive a passing score for this competency area if the coach's communication limits the thinking and learning direction for the client without specific interaction with, discussion of, and assent by the client to the limitation.[62]

HOW IS AWARENESS EVOKED?

The coach can help evoke awareness by . . .

1. Asking powerful questions that cause a client to reflect and think deeply (markers 4 & 6).
2. Making observations about the client and their situation (marker 5).
3. Directly asking the client about new insights received (markers 2 & 3).
4. Allowing for silence that provides an opportunity for the client to think and reflect.
5. Using word pictures, such as metaphor or analogy, that provide insight and new perspectives.

ASSESSOR QUESTIONS

1. Does the coach ask about insights, learnings, or take-aways during and/or at the end of the session?
2. Does the coach inquire how new awareness or learning influences the client's behavior or way of being in the situation or in perceiving himself or herself?
3. Does the coach inquire about or notice the client's emotions, body language, tone of voice, patterns of thought, or patterns of language?
4. Does the coach link the client's new learning as being a result of this coaching session or to the coaching process?
5. Does the coach invite the client to broaden the impact of this session's learning to other situations or ways of being?
6. Do the coach's questions, intuitions, and observations have the potential to create new learning for the client?
7. Does the coach ask permission to consult, teach or mentor occasionally when doing so would serve the client's immediate or longer-term agenda?
8. Does the coach's sharing of his or her own ideas, options, intuition, or wisdom have the potential to expand the client's awareness and choice points or advance the clients agenda?
9. Does the coach invite the client's comments, disagreement, or editing of the coach's contribution?[63]

SUMMARY

By being aware, the coach facilitates client insight and learning by using tools and techniques such as powerful questioning, silence, metaphor, or analogy. Evoking awareness is an important skill due to its contribution in providing new perspectives and producing personal transformation. While the old saying, "You can lead a horse to water, but you can't make him drink" is true, coaches can discover how to make clients thirsty for learning.

17

Facilitates Client Growth

ICF Core Competency 8

*The coach partners with the client to transform
learning and insight into action.
The coach promotes client autonomy
in the coaching process.*

THE ICF BELIEVES THAT coaching strives for producing personal growth and transformation in clients. Arriving at new insights and perspectives contributes greatly to growth in our clients. Facilitating client growth, along with evoking awareness, are important skills because they contribute significantly to personal transformation. At the same time, because of its subjectivity, the ability to facilitates a client's growth may be a challenging skill to develop as a coach.

In facilitating client growth, the coach . . .

1. Works with the client to integrate new awareness, insight or learning into their worldview and behaviors
2. Partners with the client to design goals, actions and accountability measures that integrate and expand new learning
3. Acknowledges and supports client autonomy in the design of goals, actions and methods of accountability

4. Supports the client in identifying potential results or learning from identified action steps
5. Invites the client to consider how to move forward, including resources, support, and potential barriers
6. Partners with the client to summarize learning and insight within or between sessions
7. Celebrates the client's progress and successes
8. Partners with the client to close the session[64]

FACILITATES CLIENT GROWTH AT EACH SKILL LEVEL

The ICF has set out specific skills and behaviors expected for Facilitates Client Growth at each of the three levels of credentials: Associate Certified Coach (ACC), Professional Certified Coach (PCC), and Master Certified Coach (MCC). In the original competencies created in 1998, three competencies were used to describe how a coach facilitates client growth: Designing Actions, Planning & Goal Setting, and Managing Progress & Accountability.[65]

KEY SKILLS EVALUATED

1. The coach's ability to support the client in exploring their learning about themselves and their situation and the application of that learning toward the client's goals
2. The coach's ability to partner fully with the client in designing actions from their new awareness, which may include thinking, feeling, or learning, that support the client in moving toward their stated agenda or goals

3. The coach's ability to support the client in developing measurable achievements that are steps toward the client's stated goals or outcomes
4. The coach's ability to partner with the client to explore and acknowledge the client's progress throughout the session
5. The coach's depth of partnership in closing the session

MINIMUM SKILL REQUIREMENTS AT THE ASSOCIATE LEVEL

At an ACC level, the minimum standard of skill that must be demonstrated to receive a passing score for competency 8 is that the coach supports the client in exploring how to apply the client's learning and awareness to post-session actions that are related to the client's stated agenda and have the potential to move the client forward in their thinking, learning, or growth. At this level, the coach may also suggest resources to assist the client in achieving their goals so long as the resources are not forced on the client.

Specifically, ACC applicants are assessed on the following skills within competency 8 as part of the performance evaluation process:

- Coach asks questions to support the client in translating awareness into action.
- Coach partners with the client to create or confirm specific action plans.
- Coach supports the client to close the session.

A coach will not receive a passing score for the Facilitates Client Growth competency on the ACC performance evaluation if the coach insists the client carry out specific actions prescribed by the coach, the coach suggests actions or steps to the client that do not have a clear relationship to the client's stated agenda, the coach does not invite the client to identify or explore how the client's learning can be applied to future actions or activities that support the client's agenda, or if the coach does not support the client to close the session.[66]

MINIMUM SKILL REQUIREMENTS AT THE PROFESSIONAL LEVEL

At the PCC level, the PCC markers are used as guidelines for minimum skills required. These markers are the skills or behaviors that can guide a coach's progress in acquiring facilitating client growth skills as one develops as a coach. There are nine markers for the Facilitates Client Growth competency.[67]

1. Coach invites or allows the client to **explore progress** toward what the client wanted to accomplish in this session.
2. Coach invites client to state or explore the client's **learning** in this session about **themself** (the who).
3. Coach invites the client to state or explore the client's **learning** in this session about their **situation** (the what).
4. Coach invites the client to consider how they will **use new learning** from this coaching session.
5. Coach partners with the client to **design** post-session thinking, reflection, or **action**.
6. Coach partners with the client to consider how to **move forward**, including resources, support, or potential barriers.
7. Coach partners with the client to design the best methods of **accountability** for themselves.

8. Coach **celebrates** the client's progress and learning.
9. Coach partners with the client on how they want to **complete** this session.

MINIMUM SKILL REQUIREMENTS AT THE MASTER LEVEL

At an MCC level, the minimum standard of skill that must be demonstrated to receive a passing score for competency 8: Facilitates Client Growth is that the coach fully partners with the client to explore the client's learning about their situation and themselves, and ways to apply new awareness to support the client's agenda, desired goals, and future growth. The coach partners with the client throughout the session to explore the client's progress and learning and supports the client in reflecting on what the client is discovering about themselves. The MCC coach demonstrates trust in the client to develop actions and accountability structures that are reflective of the client's agenda and broader learning or accomplishment that the client wants to obtain, integrate the client's strengths as well as the best of the client's learning and creating methodologies.

Specifically, MCC applicants are assessed on the following skills within competency 8: Facilitates Client Growth as part of the performance evaluation process:

- Coach checks in with client and their progress, learnings, and insights in natural and spontaneous ways throughout the session
- Coaches invites the client to sense and reflect on what they are learning about themselves
- Coach cultivates an environment for the client to intentionally apply their own learning

A coach will not receive a passing score for Facilitates Client Growth on the MCC performance evaluation if the coach does not invite full client participation or does not encourage client leadership in planning strategies, actions and methods of accountability or if the coach dominates in any way the actions or applications of learning that are created. The evaluation will also be negatively impacted if the coach does not invite or partner with the client to explore what the client is learning about themself and possible applications of that learning, or if applications of learning do not reflect a clear potential for forward movement by the client related to the client's agenda, desired outcomes, or to some other learning that the client has defined for as necessary for their growth. The evaluation will also be negatively impacted if designed plans and goals and/or discussion designed actions involves only physical activity with no attention to the thinking, learning, being, and creativity structures of the client.[68]

ASSESSOR QUESTIONS

1. Does the coach assist the client in applying and carrying forward the results of the session?
2. Does the coach test the client's level of willingness to execute the action?
3. Does the coach test the client's self-ownership of the action to ensure that the client fully owns the action commitment versus only an obligatory commitment?
4. Does the coach notice or reflect on the client's growth or changes, or invite the client to do the same?
5. Does the coach invite the client to explore progress toward what the client wanted to accomplish in this session?

6. Does the coach invite client to state or explore the client's learning in this session about themself (the who).

7. Does the coach invite the client to state or explore the client's learning in this session about their situation (the what)?

8. Does the coach invite the client to consider how they will use new learning from this coaching session?

9. Does the coach partner with the client to design post-session thinking, reflection, or action?

10. Does the coach partner with the client to consider how to move forward, including resources, support, or potential barriers?

11. Does the coach partner with the client to design the best methods of accountability for themselves?

12. Does the coach celebrate the client's progress and learning?

13. Does the coach partner with the client on how they want to complete this session?

SUMMARY

In facilitating client growth, the coach partners with the client to transform learning and insight into action. Also, the coach promotes client autonomy in the coaching process. Being able to facilitate client growth is an important skill due to its contribution in providing new perspectives and producing personal transformation. As one client responded after being asked what led to his growth as a leader, "Everything I am, I owe to my coach!"

SECTION IV

Former ICF Core Competencies and Other Coaching Skills

Former ICF Core Competencies and Other Coaching Skills

THE ORIGINAL CORE COMPETENCIES of the ICF, formulated in 1998, consisted of eleven competencies, as described in chapter 9. These were revised in 2019 and reduced to eight core competencies. The following original competencies were discontinued, and their essence disbursed among the new competencies.

- Powerful Questioning
- Direct Communication

- Designing Actions
- Planning and Goal Setting
- Managing Progress and Accountability

A chapter will be given to each of these five former competencies since they are needful and enduring skills required for masterful coaching. In addition, a chapter will be devoted to partnering in coaching since it also is an essential coaching skill.

18

Powerful Questioning

Former ICF Core Competency 6

*Powerful questioning is the ability to ask questions
that reveal the information needed for maximum benefit
to the coaching relationship and to the client.*

WHEN THE ICF CORE competencies were revised in 2019 and reduced from eleven down to eight competencies, Powerful Questioning was no longer listed as a separate competency, but rather was interspersed in other competencies, especially the Evokes Awareness competency. The descriptions in this chapter are taken from the former list of eleven competencies before the revision.

Powerful questions are:

- Clear direct questions that lead to new insight and move the client forward.
- Open-ended questions starting with *what* or *how* that are clear, direct, and succinct.

In using powerful questioning, the coach . . .

- Asks questions that reflect active listening and an understanding of the client's perspective.
- Asks questions that evoke discovery, insight, commitment, or action (e.g., those that challenge the client's assumptions).
- Asks open-ended questions that create greater clarity, possibility, or new learning.
- Asks questions that move the client toward what they desire, not questions that ask for the client to justify or look backward.

POWERFUL QUESTIONING AT EACH SKILL LEVEL

The ICF has set out specific skills and behaviors expected for powerful questioning at each of the three levels of credentials: Associate Certified Coach (ACC), Professional Certified Coach (PCC), and Master Certified Coach (MCC).[69]

MINIMUM SKILL REQUIREMENTS AT THE ASSOCIATE LEVEL

At the ACC level, the coach asks questions that attend to the client's agenda, but the questions often seek information, are formulaic, and sometimes are leading or have a "correct answer" anticipated by the coach. Typically, questions are geared to solving issues as quickly as possible that have been presented by the client.

MINIMUM SKILL REQUIREMENTS AT THE PROFESSIONAL LEVEL

At the PCC level, questions the coach asks usually attend to the client's agenda. They typically are a mix of informational and powerful questions. However, even powerful questions tend to focus on the solution. The questions likely are more responsive to the presenting agenda, rather than to any deeper needs within the client. The coach tends to use coaching terminology, versus exploring the client's language. Occasionally, leading questions appear, as well. The coach tends to ask comfortable, rather than uncomfortable questions.

The PCC markers are the skills or behaviors that can guide a coach's progress in acquiring powerful questioning skills as one develops as a coach. There were seven markers for the Powerful Questioning competency.[70]

1. The coach asks questions **about the client**, including his or her way of thinking, assumptions, beliefs, values, needs, wants, etc.
2. The coach's questions help the client explore beyond his or her current thinking to new or expanded ways of thinking about **himself or herself**.
3. The coach's questions help the client explore beyond his or her current thinking to new or expanded ways of thinking about his or her **situation**.
4. The coach's questions help the client explore beyond current thinking towards the **outcome** he or she **desires**.
5. The coach asks **clear**, direct, primarily **open-ended** questions, **one at a time**, at a pace that allows for thinking and reflection by the client.

6. The coach's questions use the **client's language** and elements of the client's learning style and frame of reference.
7. The coach's questions are **not leading**, i.e. do not contain a conclusion or direction.

MINIMUM SKILL REQUIREMENTS AT THE MASTER LEVEL

At the MCC level, the coach asks direct, evocative questions that are fully responsive to the client in the moment. These questions require significant thought by the client, and they often take the client to a new place of thinking. The coach is sensitive to the client's language and learning style in crafting questions. The coach's questions arise out of curiosity. The coach does not ask questions to which the answers already are known. The coach's questions often require the client to look deep within and get in touch with one's shadow and light sides, and so find hidden power inside. The coach asks questions that help the client create the future rather than focusing on past or even present dilemmas. The coach is not afraid of questions that will make either the coach or the client (or both) uncomfortable.

QUESTIONS TO AVOID OR USE SPARINGLY

Coaches will likely ask more powerful questions by avoiding or using only sparingly the following types of questions.

Closed Questions
Closed questions are those that can be answered with a single word or phrase. Closed questions are less effective because they limit the client's choice or expression. Closed questions tend

to shut down conversation, rather than open it up. Questions starting with the following words will invariably end up being closed questions: *Do you... Did you... Could you... Would you... Should you... Can you... Will you... Might you... Have you... Are you... Is... Was... Were... Shall...Had...* (Just for fun, try to formulate an open question starting with any of these fifteen words!) The best questions usually start with *what* or *how*, and occasionally *who* or *when* or *why*.

However, there are times when asking closed questions are appropriate. First, closed questions are useful when determining procedural matters in a coaching session:

- Are you ready to move on?
- Could I ask you a question on another subject?
- Is it time to create an action plan for this issue?
- Would you be willing to tell me more about that situation?
- Should you act on this now?

Second, closed questions are effective for clarification:

- Is this what you meant?
- Would you mind explaining what you had in mind?

Third, closed questions are useful for bottom-lining or getting a commitment from the client:

- Will you follow through on this?
- Can you finish this project by next week?
- Is this really something you want to do?

Fourth, closed questions are helpful toward the end of a coaching session in moving to a conclusion or action. At times, it is useful for a coach to help clients limit the scope of their exploration and begin to decide on specific directions. The coach might offer closed coaching questions that invite a client's decision and action:

- Do you want to decide on some actions right away, or is this still a little early for you?
- Do you prefer option A, option B, or option C?
- Are you going to respond right away, or do you want to let the situation settle down first?

The coach needs to ask closed questions judiciously, making sure that the question is not suggesting a direction or solution that the client has not already surfaced. Nor should the closed question mask the coach's impatience for the client to make a decision and move on.

Having trouble turning closed into open questions? Here is a sure-fire way. Simply insert the phrase "To what extent" at the beginning of the question! For example:

Closed	Open
• Are you happy about this decision?	To what extent are you happy about this decision?
• Does your spouse agree?	To what extent does your spouse agree?
• Are you living up to your full potential?	To what extent are you living up to your full potential?

Leading Questions
Leading questions are the kind that lawyers use in cross-examining a witness during a trial. Leading questions are opinion statements disguised as questions. As such, they try to put words in the other person's mouth. Therefore, they are manipulative Leading questions almost always are closed questions. Here are some examples. Note that the phrase changing it from a statement into a question can be used at either the beginning or the end of the sentence.

- Isn't it true that...
- Wouldn't you say that...
- Isn't it right that...
- Can't we agree that...
- The truth is . . . , isn't that right?

From the coach's perspective, the purpose of asking a question is to obtain new information or generate new ideas. To do this well, it is important that the wording of the question does not disguise an attempt by the coach to influence, lead, or guide the content of the answer in a certain direction. Therefore, leading questions are entirely inappropriate to use in a coaching context.

"Are you angry?" is an example of a more subtle leading question. While the client may indeed be angry, there may be other emotions involved, such as sadness or fear. Drawing attention to that one emotion may be giving it unnecessary weight. A more neutral question would be "What are you feeling?"

Directive or Answer-in-the-Question
This type of question is not quite as blatant as the leading question in trying to push the coach's agenda or solution on

the client. However, it does violate the spirit of coaching in that it suggests a solution for the client's problem. Here are some examples.

- How soon will you have a face-to-face talk to resolve this conflict with her?
- Have you thought about firing him?
- Obviously, your finances are in bad shape, so what is your plan to increase your income?
- Since attempts at reconciliation have not worked, how soon do you want to file for a divorce?
- With your health at risk, how fast do you think you could lose thirty pounds?

Coaches who provide clients with suggested solutions risk two things. First, they risk robbing the client of solving their own problem and taking personal responsibility for their own life. Second, the coach risks being blamed if the solution does not work. Thus, coaching questions that offer a totally open field for client response are neutral questions. They are considered much more useful to help broaden client perspectives.

Judgment Questions

Judgment questions can be even more subtle than leading questions or directive questions. Judgment questions show a lack of complete acceptance by the coach. They can seriously damage the coaching relationship in that they demonstrate prejudice or negativity on the part of the coach toward the client. Here are some examples.

- How has your negative attitude impacted this situation?
- When are you going to start making some real money?

- How could you be less of a dictator in your leadership style?
- What would it take for you to be more of a team player at work?
- Why are you so lazy?

Why Questions

Why questions should be used carefully and sparingly for three reasons. First, they can question a person's motives and judgments, resulting in the client seeing such questions as a subtle form of punishment. Second, they tend to look at the past rather than focus on the future. This is based on the notion that to succeed one must understand why they failed. (For example, is it important in learning to swim, to analyze why a person almost drowned?) In effect, why questions only let clients meander within their same old limited past frame of reference. Third, they tend to invite an intellectual analytical response rather than a response from the heart.

Negative Interrogation

Negative questions focus clients on their blocks and hindrances, such as:

- Why don't you . . .
- What keeps you from . . .
- What are the things hindering you from completing this action?

Other more positive-oriented coaching questions will help your clients move forward in finding and designing their solutions.

Complicated (Run-On) and Multiple Questions

At times a coach may ask a question and then sense that the question was not clear. The coach attempts to clarify it by adding more and more to the question. Doing so results in a long run-on question that confuses the client. A similar mistake is to fire multiple questions at clients without giving them the chance to answer any of them.

The most powerful questions often are short, simple, and to the point. The coach uses words that the client will understand without having to struggle over their meaning. Some of the best questions are stand-alone questions, and the coach allows time for the client to ponder and give a thoughtful response.

Information-Gathering Questions

Beginning coaches often think it is their responsibility to propose answers or to offer options and solutions to their client. This results in them asking more and more questions about various details regarding the issue. The reality is that many clients have already given significant thought to the issue facing them. And they may well be an expert in their field. The likelihood is very slim that the coach will offer an option the client has not already considered.

The client does not need a new option, but a new perspective. The coach's responsibility is to ask a powerful question that causes a shift in the client's thinking, so that the issue is seen in a whole new light. The new perspective allows the client to view the issue from a different angle, so that new options come to mind.

To Sum it Up

The effective coach uses powerful questions to help clients discover and grow. In most cases, the wise coach will avoid using closed questions, leading questions, judgmental question, directive questions, negative, and run-on questions.

HOW DOES A COACH ASK POWERFUL QUESTIONS?

Here are some suggestions.

1. *Powerful questions generally are open-ended questions.*
   Open-ended questions are those that cannot be answered with yes or no. Open questions require clients to reflect and to express their thoughts verbally. Someone once observed, "Open questions are the single sure practice that invites critical thinking and learning."

2. *Powerful questions are for the benefit of the client, rather than the coach.*
   It is tempting for a coach to ask information-gathering questions, thinking that they need more background to help solve the client's problem. At such times, the coach needs to be reminded that it's their job to help the client find their own solution. Before asking a question, ask yourself, "Am I asking this question for my benefit or for the benefit of my client?"

3. *Powerful questions stimulate the client toward clarity, discovery, insight, and action, rather than serving to correct the client.*
   Coaches make better progress with clients when they choose an accepting, non-judgmental attitude. Such an attitude precludes the need to correct clients. Instead, questions should be designed to help clients make discoveries and new insights that lead to positive actions.

4. *Powerful questions are usually forward-looking, not backward-looking.*
Whereas much of counseling dwells on the past, coaching is future oriented. Coaches help clients arrive at new solutions, envision bigger dreams, and arrive at new possibilities. Powerful questions tend to help clients focus on the future, rather than upon the past.

5. *Powerful questions arise out of active listening and are based upon the client's agenda.*
The best questions are not planned but are created out of the moment in a coaching session. The coach listens well and formulates questions based on the context of the discussion and the client's agenda.

6. *Powerful questions are neutral and come from a non-judgmental heart.*
Questions that are judgmental or negative tear down and disempower rather than motivate and inspire. The best questions are neutral in that they contain no prejudices, directives, or leanings on the part of the coach.

7. *Powerful questions are short, simple and to the point.*

- What do you want?
- Where are we?
- What's next?
- Where do you want to go?
- What do you see?
- What did you learn?
- What will you do?
- When will you do it?
- What do *you* think?

8. *Powerful questions arise out of curiosity.*
    Curious questions are open ended with a broad focus that invite consideration of issues not previously thought of but still leave the client in control. Curious questions are used for the purpose of clarifying an issue and for broadening the scope of the discussion.

9. *Powerful questions can come from intuition or a hunch.*
    Intuitive questions are based upon a hunch or a sixth sense as a response to what one may be hearing or seeing. At times, when using an intuitive question one may sense spiritual guidance. While an intuitive question sometimes can lead to a breakthrough, the coach should be careful in how the question is worded. Keep in mind these suggestions:

    *   Do not present your hunch as an absolute fact, but just as something to be explored.
    *   Word it in a soft, tentative way.
    *   Use phrases such as "I wonder about..." or "I'm curious as to whether..."

10. *Powerful questions can be 360-degree questions.*
    Powerful questions can explore issues from many various angles that help broaden the client's perspective and increase insight. For example:

    *   *Background*: "Step back for a moment and tell me, what are the underlying issues?"
    *   *Systemic*: "What other factors are influencing this issue?"
    *   *Result*: "What result would you like to have from this situation?"

- *Culture*: "In what ways might culture be involved?"
- *Personal growth*: "What inner changes would you like to see for yourself?"
- *Interpersonal*: "What relationship dynamics do you see at work?"
- *Emotional*: "What emotions are coming into play here?"
- *Financial*: "How are concerns over money issues impacting this situation?"
- *Spiritual*: "What spiritual factors might be at work in this situation?"
- *Family*: "How are family dynamics and relationships impacting the issue?"
- *Strategy*: "What are the first steps to take in working on this?"

11. *Powerful questions are usually stand-alone questions.*
   Questions that begin with *and* or *so* indicate a link to previous aspects of the conversation. Powerful questions can stand alone. All it takes for a breakthrough in a coaching session is one powerful question that totally changes the client's perspective and provides a new outlook on a situation.

12. *Powerful questions have a practical orientation, rather than a theoretical bent.*
   Asking practical questions, such as "What result do you want to take away from our conversation today?" are especially useful at the beginning of a coaching sequence. This question will help focus the conversation so that precise action steps are created by the end of the session. When clients approach issues using general or vague theoretical language, it is helpful for coaches to bring them back

to precise, measurable situations or specific people and places. Consider the following:

Client: "I can't seem to finish my projects."
Coach: "Can you give a precise example of an ongoing project you would like to finish?"

Client: "I cannot stand indecisive people."
Coach: "Who in your life today is an indecisive person?"

13. *Powerful questions usually start with* what *or* how.
Powerful questions encourage clients to envision future possibilities, and questions starting with *what* or *how* (such as, "What will you . . . ?" or "How will you go about . . . ?") tend to accomplish this best results. Once a goal or an action plan has been agreed upon, then using questions that start with *when, where* or *who* help pin down the details of the plan.

14. *Powerful questions have the appropriate linguistic emphasis.*
Consider the differences in meaning in the following questions:

- **What** do you want?
- What **do** you want?
- What do **you** want?
- What do you **want**?

MAKE QUESTIONS GO DEEPER

Powerful questions have the power to transform lives. Experienced coaches consider how to form questions that go deeper. Note how in these examples each question goes to a deeper level. Frequently poor questions are closed, so the first step is making it open-ended.

- Is this what you want?
  - o *Open*: What do you want?
  - o *Better*: What do you really, really want?
  - o *Best*: How does the life you are living line up with your core values?
- Is this the honest thing to do?
  - o *Open*: What is the honest thing to do?
  - o *Better*: What would your closest friends think about you if they knew this?
  - o *Best*: If you carried through on this, what would your conscience say about doing so?

ASSESSOR QUESTIONS

1. Does the coach ask clear questions that help the client explore issues, his or her role, behaviors, and being?
2. Does the coach ask questions that encourage thinking in new ways, that help a client move toward his or her desired outcome?
3. Do the coach's questions demonstrate inquiring about thinking, assumptions, beliefs, and values (without necessarily using those exact words in the coaching)?
4. Do the coach's questions and observations at times challenge the client's thinking?
5. Do the coach's question and observations move the client out of the current story he or she is telling and help the client look forward?
6. Does the coach invite the client to see the situation from a different angle or to look at the situation from a different perspective?

7. Does the coach ask questions that help the client reframe a problem, or challenge him or her to create a more empowering picture?

8. Does the coach ask the client to imagine or picture or articulate his/her desired future?

9. Does the coach ask the client to work backward from the future to the present?

10. Does the coach use the miracle question or the "magic wand" question (solutions focus)? (For example, "if I were to waive a magic wand that solved this issue, what would the result look like?)

11. Do the coach's questions assist the client to create new scenarios that would engender success for his or her goals?

12. Does the coach ask questions that provoke inquiry, questions that cannot be answered simply with a yes or a no?

13. Does the coach allow the client to think before inserting another question?

14. After asking a question, does the coach allow a time of silence for the client to think?

15. Does the coach refrain from using double or triple questioning (stacked questions)?

16. Does the coach understand and work with the client's learning style?[71]

SUMMARY

Powerful questioning is the ability to ask questions that reveal the information needed for maximum benefit to the coaching relationship and to the client. The principles presented here form the foundation for asking powerful questions. Remember that it is not necessary in a coaching session to ask one powerful question after another. Doing so actually dilutes their impact. Rather, one or two powerful questions can change the course of the conversation, enable the client to gain a new perspective, and grasp possibilities previously unseen. A powerful question usually takes a client by surprise and puts him or her off balance. When faced with a truly powerful question, their immediate reaction often is silence. You'll know that you've asked a powerful question when the client looks stunned and withdraws on an inner quest.

19

Direct Communication

Former ICF Core Competency 7

Direct communication is the skill of easily and freely sharing observations, intuitions, and feedback with the client without being attached to one's comments.

DIRECT COMMUNICATION WAS ONE of the original eleven core competencies created in 1998. In November 2019, the ICF released an updated version of the competencies. Direct Communication was no longer listed as a distinct competency but was incorporated into other competencies, notably the Evokes Awareness competency. While it now is not regarded as a separate competency, Direct Communication is a coaching skill still frequently used by masterful coaches. According to the ICF, direct communication is "the ability to communicate effectively during coaching sessions, and to use language that has the greatest positive impact on the client." [72]

Direct communication ...

- Is clear, articulate, and straightforward in sharing and providing feedback.
- Helps the client understand from another perspective what he or she wants or is uncertain about.

- Clearly states coaching objectives, meeting agenda, and purpose of techniques or exercises.
- Uses language appropriate and respectful to the client (e.g., non-sexist, non-racist, non-technical, non-jargon).
- Uses metaphor and analogy to help to illustrate a point or paint a verbal picture[73]

DIRECT COMMUNICATION AT EACH SKILL LEVEL

The ICF has set out specific skills and behaviors expected for direct communication at each of the three levels of credentials: ACC (Associate Certified Coach), PCC (Professional Certified Coach), and MCC (Master Certified Coach).[74]

MINIMUM SKILL REQUIREMENTS AT THE ASSOCIATE LEVEL

At the ACC level, the coach sometimes is fairly direct, but usually uses too many words or feels a need to "dress up" a question or observation. Questions and observations often contain vocabulary from the coach's training. Most communication occurs on a very safe level for the coach.

MINIMUM SKILL REQUIREMENTS AT THE PROFESSIONAL LEVEL

At the PCC level, the coach usually is direct, but at times feels a need to "dress up" a question or an observation. The coach occasionally treats his/her intuition as the truth. The coach sometimes does not say what is occurring for the coach for fear that the client is not open to hearing it. The coach also may evidence a need to soften communication for fear of being wrong. The coach tends to use some coaching language versus the language of the client. The coach has a sufficient but not a broad base of language tools to use with the client.

The PCC markers are the skills or behaviors that can guide a coach's progress in acquiring direct communication skills as one develops as a coach. There were six markers for the Direct Communication competency.[75]

1. The coach **shares observations**, intuitions, comments, thoughts, and feelings to serve the client's learning or forward movement.
2. The coach shares observations, intuitions, comments, thoughts, and feelings **without** any **attachment** to them being right.
3. The coach uses the **client's language** or language that reflects the client's way of speaking.
4. The coach's language is generally **clear** and **concise**.
5. The coach allows the **client** to do most of the **talking**.
6. The coach allows the client to complete speaking **without interrupting** unless there is a stated coaching purpose to do so.

MINIMUM SKILL REQUIREMENTS AT THE MASTER LEVEL

At the MCC level, the coach easily and freely shares one's perceptions without attachment. The coach shares directly and simply and often incorporates the client's language. The coach fully trusts the client to choose the responses to the coach's communication that is best for the client. The coach invites, respects, and celebrates direct communication back from the client. The coach creates sufficient space for the client to have more communication time than the coach. The coach has a broad language base to use and employ, and the coach uses the client's language to broaden that base.

Direct communication is a challenging skill to use well. Dr. Val Hastings, MCC, founder of the coaching school Coaching4Clergy, states, "I have never observed an ACC level coach using direct communication correctly." Warning: beginning coaches should use direct communication sparingly, due to the potential for offending the client with misuse. Keith Webb, founder of Creative Results Management coaching school, said, "We don't teach direct communication in our school until the second year because so many beginning coaches approach it all wrong."[76]

SHARING OBSERVATIONS IN DIRECT COMMUNICATION

In most cases, direct communication is best limited to sharing reflections regarding what the coach is observing about the client in the coaching session or about the client's situation. Sharing observations is often where beginning coaches get into trouble! A word of caution—do it sparingly. When you share observations, keep these things in mind.

Sharing observations *usually is* . . .

- Sharing what you are experiencing in the conversation or relationship.
- Sharing what you are noticing about the client during the conversation.
- Sharing what you are noticing about the client's situation.
- Sharing feedback.

- Bottom-lining issues.

Sharing observations *usually is not* . . .

- Sharing ideas.
- Teaching methods.
- Giving advice.
- Telling stories.

When sharing observations there are some dos and don'ts every coach should know.

Do

- Attend to the client's agenda.
- Be concise—try for seven words or less.
- Share what you are observing about the client during the conversation.
- Share what you are observing about the client's situation.
- Share to expand dialogue and thinking, rather than limiting them.
- Share freely, without attachment to the outcome, trusting the client's response.
- Share beyond the present situation to below-the-surface patterns and broader thinking.
- Invite the client to share their intuition and mental models.
- Avoid attachment to a particular outcome or solution.

Fast Track to Masterful Coaching

Don't:

- Provide long explanations.
- Be indirect or hint.
- Judge.
- Change the agenda without discussion and permission from the client.

HOW TO AVOID ATTACHMENT

Being attached to your point of view or to a particular outcome is detrimental to a coach. To avoid attachment when sharing observations, feedback, or ideas, have this attitude and say to the client: "You can take it, leave it, or modify it. It's up to you." Realize from the start that for whatever reason, the other person may not want to follow your suggestion and be okay with that. Leave the choice with them.

Here's a three-step process to share advice, feedback, or ideas without attachment:

1. *Share it briefly.* In coaching we try to keep our feedback or observations to one sentence.
2. *Ask how they see it.* Follow-up your feedback or observation with a question to engage the person in a discussion.
3. *Let it go.* It's up to the other person to do something with your suggestion. That's his or her choice. And depending on their actions you can choose how to further engage with this person. That's your choice.

If your observation is of a sensitive nature, a beginning step is helpful. Soften it by acknowledging that you could be wrong and inviting their push back.

I had been coaching a client for eight months and noticed that whenever things did not go right, he deflected blame onto someone else rather than taking responsibility. I determined that it would be in his best interest if I shared that observation with him. At our next coaching conversation, this is what I said. "Jim (not his real name), I could be wrong about this, so I invite your pushback. What I've noticed is that each time something does not go right, you seem to place blame on others rather than accepting responsibility for it yourself.

How does it seem to you?"

If you find yourself trying to explain your point of view or convince the client, then you're attached. You may think the other person does not understand your idea and thar's why there is resistance, but remember people evaluate their situation with different criteria than our own. They have their own values and priorities. Leave the choice up to the other person. Share your observations, feedback or ideas and let it go.

ASSESSOR QUESTIONS

1. Does the majority of the coach's sharing have the potential to serve the client's forward movement?
2. Do the coach's statements help the client explore beyond his or her current thinking to new or expanded ways of thinking?
3. Do the coach's statements help the client explore beyond current thinking towards the outcome he or she desires?
4. Do some of the coach's questions and observations challenge the client's thinking?
5. When the coach shares beliefs and assessments, are they stated as those of the coach rather than held as absolute truths?

6. When sharing observations, intuition, comments, thoughts, or feelings, does the coach clearly communicate that they are there for the client to respond to in any way he or she chooses?

7. Does the coach use the client's language, words, speech patterns, rate of speech, etc., as well as introducing new language?

8. When sharing observations, intuitions, comments, thoughts, or feelings, does the coach clearly communicate and articulate in a manner that is easily and readily understood by the client?

9. Does the coach talk significantly less than the client in the totality of the conversation?

10. Does the coach refrain from interrupting the client during the session?

11. If the coach interrupts on one or two occasions, does she or he provide a stated purpose for doing so? [77]

SUMMARY

Direct communication is the skill of easily and freely sharing observations, intuitions, and feedback with the client without being attached to one's comments. Direct communication is primarily sharing observations about the client noticed in the conversation or about their situation. A key to sharing without attachment is to be brief, invite feedback, and be willing to let it go. Direct communication is a difficult coaching skill to learn, so beginning coaches should use direct communication sparingly, due to the potential for offending the client with misuse.

20

Designing Actions

Former ICF Core Competency 9

Designing actions is the ability to create with the client opportunities for ongoing learning, during coaching and in work/life situations, and for taking new actions that will most effectively lead to agreed-upon coaching results.

IN DESIGNING ACTIONS, the coach . . .

- Works with the client to design actions or activities (fieldwork) outside of the coaching session to continue exploration, increase awareness and learning, and move toward the desired goal.
- Works with the client to design actions that support the client's goals, learning style, and desired pace.
- Brainstorms and assists the client to define actions that will enable the client to demonstrate, practice, and deepen new learning.
- Helps the client to focus on and systematically explore specific concerns and opportunities that are central to agreed-upon coaching goals.
- Engages the client to explore alternative ideas and solutions, to evaluate options, and to make related decisions.

- Promotes active experimentation and self-discovery, where the client applies what has been discussed and learned during sessions immediately afterward in his or her work or life setting.
- Celebrates client successes and capabilities for future growth.
- Challenges client's assumptions and perspectives to provoke new ideas and find new possibilities for action.
- Advocates or brings forward points of view that are aligned with client goals and, without attachment, engages the client to consider them.
- Helps the client act on his or her decisions soon after the coaching session, providing immediate support.
- Encourages, stretches, and challenges, but also recognizes a comfortable pace of learning.[78]

DESIGNING ACTIONS AT EACH SKILL LEVEL

The ICF has set out specific skills and behaviors expected for Designing Actions at each of the three levels of credentials: Associate Certified Coach (ACC), Professional Certified Coach (PCC), and Master Certified Coach (MCC).[79]

MINIMUM SKILL REQUIREMENTS AT THE ASSOCIATE LEVEL

At the ACC level, the coach continues to suggest homework and actions that they think would best handle the problem or achieve the goal. Actions tend to be one-dimensional in nature. The coach encourages taking new actions that will most effectively lead to agreed-upon coaching results.

MINIMUM SKILL REQUIREMENTS AT THE PROFESSIONAL LEVEL

At the PCC level, the coach engages in some, but not a complete partnership with the client, to develop actions. Again, the actions are attuned to solving the situational issue the client has presented, rather than looking beyond the situation to other, broader learning that might be inherent in the situation. The PCC level coach tends to define forward motion only in terms of physical action.

THE PCC MARKERS

The PCC markers are the skills or behaviors that can guide a coach's progress in acquiring designing actions skills as one develops as a coach. Those who designed the PCC markers chose to combine the final three core competencies, making a list of six markers. Markers 2 and 3 focus on the Designing Actions competency.[80]

- The coach assists the client to **design** what **actions/** thinking the client will do after the session in order for the client to continue moving toward the client's desired outcomes.
- The coach invites or allows the client to consider her or his **path forward**, including, as appropriate, **support** mechanisms, **resources,** and potential **barriers**.

MINIMUM SKILL REQUIREMENTS AT THE MASTER LEVEL

At the MCC level, the coach works in complete partnership with the client to design actions or, in the alternative, lets the client lead in designing actions. The coach and client design actions that fit the client's goals, learning style, and pace of wanted or necessary movement. The coach allows actions to include thinking, creating, and doing. The coach engages the client in relating designed actions to other aspects of what the client wants, thereby broadening the scope of learning and growth. The coach encourages informed experimentation to help the client develop more powerful, leveraged actions.

ASSESSOR QUESTIONS

1. Does the coach assist the client in applying and carrying forward the results of the session?
2. Does the coach encourage a broad range of actions that may include . . .
   - Further thinking?
   - Additional feeling or living with an idea?
   - Self-inquiry?
   - Behavior change?
   - Task completion?
   - Research?
   - Experimentation?
   - Building a habit?
   - Practicing an intention?
3. Does the coach assist the client in clarifying and planning a timeline around various commitments?
4. Does the coach explore the likelihood of an action to occur in the future, such as in the use of a scaling question? (For example: "On a scale of 1 to 10, how likely are you to complete this action step before we talk next time?")
5. Does the coach inquire concerning the client's feelings about the action?

6. Does the coach test the client's level of willingness to execute the action?
7. Does the coach test the client's self-ownership of the action to ensure that the client fully owns the action commitment versus only an obligatory commitment?
8. Does the coach inquire about or identify potential obstacles to carrying out an action, and help the client plan against them?
9. Does the coach not force the conversation regarding action steps and commitment, if the client indicates that she or he does not need that conversation?[81]

SUMMARY

Designing actions is the ability to create with the client opportunities for ongoing learning, during coaching and in work/life situations, and for taking new actions that will most effectively lead to agreed-upon coaching results. Actions steps often arise out of the context of the coaching conversation. A simple, but effective question is, What actions could you take to move forward? Both coach and client would do well to remember the saying, Progress, not perfection.

21

Planning and Goal Setting

Former ICF Core Competency 10

Planning and goal setting is the ability to develop and maintain an effective coaching plan with the client.

TWO ASPECTS OF COMPETENCY 10 involve planning and goal setting for the immediate session and for the longer term. Early in each coaching conversation a goal is set for what the client wants to accomplish in the session. This goal is what is called the result phase, or in ICF terminology the Coaching Agreement competency. Long-range goals are also set that may take weeks or months to reach. Some of these goals are set during the contracting when the coach and client have their first meeting. Some call these series goals. Other long-range goals are set during the course of coaching conversations, as it becomes clear to clients that these would be worthwhile goals.

In planning and goal setting, the coach . . .

- Partners with the client to develop goals that are SMART (specific, measurable, achievable, relevant, with a time frame).
- Stays aware of the client's plan, learning style, pace, and commitment to the goal.

- Identifies and targets early successes that are important to the client.
- Consolidates collected information and establishes a coaching plan and development goals with the client that address concerns and major areas for learning and development.
- Adjusts plans as warranted by the coaching process and by changes in the situation.
- Helps the client identify and access different resources for learning, such as books or other professionals.[82]

PLANNING & GOAL SETTING AT EACH SKILL LEVEL

The ICF has set out specific skills and behaviors expected for Planning and Goal Setting at each of the three levels of credentials: Associate Certified Coach (ACC), Professional Certified Coach (PCC), and Master Certified Coach (MCC).[83]

MINIMUM SKILL REQUIREMENTS AT THE ASSOCIATE LEVEL

At the ACC level, the coach tends to adopt goals suggested by the client at their most obvious level. Planning and goal setting tend to be one dimensional in nature, with the coach sometimes substituting his/her expertise for the client.

MINIMUM SKILL REQUIREMENTS AT THE PROFESSIONAL LEVEL

At the PCC level, the coach engages in some partnering with the client, although not a complete partnership, to develop goals and plans. The actions are attuned to solving the situational issue the client has presented, rather than looking beyond the situation to other, broader learning that might be inherent in the situation. The PCC level coach tends to edit plans presented by the client.

The PCC markers are the skills or behaviors that can guide a coach's progress in acquiring planning and goal setting skills as one develops as a coach. Those who designed the PCC markers chose to combine the final three core competencies, making a list of six markers. Markers 3 and 5 focus on the Planning and Goal Setting competency.[84]

- The coach invites or allows the client to consider her or his **path forward**, including, as appropriate, **support** mechanisms, **resources,** and potential **barriers**.
- The coach partners with the client to close the session.

MINIMUM SKILL REQUIREMENTS AT THE MASTER LEVEL

At the MCC level, the coach works with the client to clarify and develop goals that achieve more than just the presenting concerns of the client. The coach lets the client lead in designing goals and planning or, in the alternative, works in complete partnership with the client to create goals and plans. The coach and client create goals and plans that fit the client's goals, learning style, and pace of movement. The coach encourages plans to include thinking, creating, and doing. The coach engages the client in relating goals and plans to other aspects of what the client wants, thereby broadening the scope of learning and growth.

MAKING GOALS SMART

Clients will be more likely to complete goals that are SMART. This acronym stands for Specific, Measurable, Achievable, Relevant and has a Time frame. (Some substitute Attractive and Realistic. Others add an S for Significant.) Once clients have arrived at a goal, it will become clearer if the coach walks them through to make it a SMART goal. An important additional step is to add the phrase *so that*. This phrase forces them to define what it is they really want to accomplish.

After writing the goal, check to make sure that all of the SMART aspects are included by asking the client:

- Is this a significant goal, worthy of your time and energy?
- What is the specific, concrete, tangible part of this goal?
- Is it measurable? What numbers are present? How will you know that the goal has been accomplished?
- Is the goal realistic and achievable? Is it really possible to do?
- Is the goal relevant to your life, your vision, and your values? Why is this goal important to you?
- Is there a date or time frame by when the goal must be reached?
- Is this the right time to accomplish this goal, or are there other factors that must be dealt with first?

If you wish to have clients really think more deeply through the process of setting a goal, incorporate the SNOW process (Small Notes On Wall) before writing the SMART goal.

- Using stickie notes, brainstorm all the possible ways to address the issue. Put just one idea on each sheet and try to list twenty-five to thirty possible solutions.
- Group the stickie notes into related categories. Give each category a title.
- Imagine that you are writing a book about these options. Write a title for this book that encompasses what you want to see happen.

This process will cause the client to think more deeply and arrive at a well-thought-out SMART goal.

Not all action steps need to be written as SMART goals. However, those action steps that are more complicated, more important, and will take longer to accomplish will benefit from being worded as SMART action steps.

ASSESSOR QUESTIONS

1. Does the coach inquire about the client's perception of how well the conversation is achieving this session's goal?
2. Does the coach follow up on the client's stated perception of how well the conversation is achieving this session's goal?
3. Does the coach partner with the client to close the session by inviting the client to consider how s/he wants to complete the session?
4. Does the coach check with the client on what topics the client is complete with and on what may need to be carried to the next session, or what the client might work on outside the session?

5. Does the coach check with the client to ensure that s/he is complete with the conversation before ending the session?[85]

SUMMARY

Planning and goal setting is the ability to develop and maintain an effective coaching plan with the client. In planning and goal setting, the coach partners with the client to develop SMART goals. The coach stays aware of the client's plan, learning style, pace, and commitment to the goal. Goals can be both immediate, such as the session goal for today's conversation, or long-range, which may take weeks or months to achieve. Goals are set during the initial contracting session for the coaching relationship, as well as along the way during any session.

22

Managing Progress and Accountability

Former Core Competency 11

Managing progress and accountability is the ability to hold attention on what is important for the client, and to leave responsibility with the client to take action.[86]

WHEN MANAGING PROGRESS AND accountability, the coach . . .

- Stays focused on what is important for the client and holds him/her accountable.
- Clearly requests of the client actions that will move the client toward his or her stated goals.
- Demonstrates follow through by asking the client about those actions that the client committed to during the previous session(s).
- Acknowledges the client for what they have done, have not done, and have learned or become aware of since the previous coaching session(s).
- Effectively prepares, organizes, and reviews with the client information obtained during sessions.
- Keeps the client on track between sessions by holding attention on the coaching plan and outcomes, agreed-upon courses of action, and topics for future session(s).

- Focuses on the coaching plan, but also is open to adjusting behaviors and actions based on the coaching process and shifts in direction during sessions.
- Is able to move back and forth between the big picture of where the client is heading, setting a context for what is being discussed, and where the client wishes to go.
- Promotes client's self-discipline and holds the client accountable for what they say they are going to do, for the results of an intended action, or for a specific plan with related time frames.
- Develops the client's ability to make decisions, address key concerns, and develop himself or herself (to get feedback, to determine priorities and set the pace of learning, to reflect on and learn from experiences).
- Positively confronts the client with the fact that he or she did not take agreed-upon actions when necessary.[87]

MANAGING PROGRESS AND ACCOUNTABILITY AT EACH SKILL LEVEL

The ICF has set out specific skills and behaviors expected for Managing Progress and Accountability at each of the three levels of credentials: Associate Certified Coach (ACC), Professional Certified Coach (PCC), and Master Certified Coach (MCC).[88]

MINIMUM SKILL REQUIREMENTS AT THE ASSOCIATE LEVEL

At the ACC level, the coach tends to suggest forms of accountability that may feel a bit parental in nature. Accountability tends to be one dimensional.

MINIMUM SKILL REQUIREMENTS AT THE PROFESSIONAL LEVEL

At the PCC level, the coach partners with the client in some ways in developing methods of accountability. Those methods often reflect tools learned in the coach's training school.

The PCC markers are the skills or behaviors that can guide a coach's progress in acquiring managing progress and accountability skills as one develops as a coach. Those who designed the PCC markers chose to combine the final three core competencies, making a list of six markers. Markers 1, 4, and 6 focus on the Managing Progress and Accountability competency.[89]

- The coach invites or allows client to explore **progress** toward what he or she wants to accomplish **in the session**.
- The coach assists the client to design the best methods of **accountability** for herself or himself.
- The coach notices and reflects the client's **progress**.

MINIMUM SKILL REQUIREMENTS AT THE MASTER LEVEL

At the MCC level, the coach has the client determine their own methods of accountability, and the coach offers support for those methods. The client determines who should be on their accountability team and how to use each person, including the coach. The coach trusts the client to be accountable to him/herself and lovingly calls the client to account if agreed-upon forward movement has not occurred.

VALUE OF MANAGING PROGRESS AND ACCOUNTABILITY

The fieldwork aspect of coaching is the focus of this competency. It highlights the overall direction and drive of coaching. This competency underscores what makes coaching a unique form of helping, being pivotal in forming sustainable change. It requires the coach to partner with the client to develop clear measures of success and accountability that support the client's goals, and therefore move the client forward. Following up on action steps in the coaching session helps both client and coach applaud successes, reframe uncompleted actions as learning opportunities, and create the evolving agenda. The coach is consistent with accountability, but leaves responsibility with the client to follow through on actions in between sessions.

ASSESSOR QUESTIONS

1. Does the coach inquire about the client's progress toward this session's goal?
2. Does the coach inquire about the client's progress toward longer-term goals?
3. Does the coach follow up on the client's stated progress toward the goal, or lack of progress toward the goal?
4. Does the coach assist the client in designing the best methods of accountability for her/himself?
5. Does the coach occasionally agree to serve as an accountability partner for the client?
6. Does the coach inquire about other forms of support for client accountability structures?
7. Does the coach inquire about self-accountability structures?

8. Does the coach follow up on the client's stated commitments from previous coaching sessions?
9. Does the coach celebrate the client's success when he or she executes on agreed-upon action commitments?
10. Does the coach inquire about obstacles that got in the way of the client's efforts to follow through on actions?
11. Does the coach express willingness to review the client's progress at the next upcoming session?
12. Does the coach offer additional support between sessions, as warranted by the coaching agreement contract?
13. Does the coach notice and reflect on the client's progress toward desired outcomes, or invite the client to do the same?
14. Does the coach notice or reflect on the client's growth or changes, or invite the client to do the same?[90]

SUMMARY

Managing progress and accountability is the ability to hold attention on what is important for the client, and to leave responsibility with the client to take action. The coach stays focused on what is important for the client and holds him or her accountable. This competency focuses on fieldwork or action steps, with the coach agreeing to check with the client on what has been accomplished and what has not. The accountability factor is a driving force to move the client forward toward achieving desired goals.

23

Partnering with Clients

How to Partner with Clients in a Coaching Conversation

PARTNERING WITH CLIENTS IS a basic skill required for masterful coaching. The fact that partnering is mentioned frequently in the ICF documents that describe masterful coaching is evidence of its importance.

How frequently is partnering mentioned?

Core Competencies	=	17 times
PCC markers	=	16 times
MCC minimum skills requirements	=	40 times

Various definitions of coaching show that partnering is essential to coaching.

- Coaching is **partnering** with clients in a thought-provoking and creative process that inspires them to maximize their personal and professional potential. (ICF)[91]
- Coaching is a **partnership** that accelerates what is already underway or about to begin, that maximizes potential, moving people from good to great.[92]

- Coaching is a non-directive intentional conversation in which a person **partners** with another to help them gain clarity or new perspectives.

WHAT DOES IT MEAN TO PARTNER?

Here are some dictionary definitions of partnering.[93]

- Being united or associated with another in an activity or a sphere of common interest
- Being united in a relationship with another
- Sharing an intimate relationship with another

In coaching, partnering has a specialized meaning. "In essence, exhibiting a partnering behavior means that *a coach invites the client to make choices.*"[94]

HOW TO PARTNER

Whenever the coach places the client in a position of making a choice, this is partnering. For example, to arrive at the coaching agreement, the coach might ask one of these questions:

- What would you like to work on today?
- What are you bringing to our session today?
- How are you coming to our conversation today?
- What would you like to achieve from our work together in this session?
- What do you want to focus on today?
- Where would you like us to begin from in today's session?

All of these questions illustrate partnering with the client, since they invite the client to make a choice.

WAYS OF PARTNERING

The core competencies give specific ways to partner with a client, no matter the level of certification.

ACC SKILLS[95]

- Evokes Awareness (descriptive statement # 5) – Invites the client to share more about their experience in the moment.
- Evokes Awareness (descriptive statement # 9) – Invites the client to generate ideas about how they can move forward and what they are willing or able to do.
- Facilitates Client Growth (descriptive statement # 5) – Invites the client to consider how to move forward, including resources, support, and potential barriers.

PCC MARKERS[96]

- Cultivates Trust and Safety (marker # 4) – Coach partners with the client by inviting the client to respond in any way to the coach's contributions and accepts the client's response.
- Evokes Awareness (marker # 5) – Encourages the coach to share—with no attachment—observations, intuitions, comments, thoughts, or feelings, and invites the client's exploration through verbal or tonal invitation.
- Facilitates Client Growth (marker # 1) – Coach invites or allows the client to explore progress toward what the client wanted to accomplish in this session.

- Facilitates Client Growth (marker # 2) – Coach invites the client to state or explore the client's learning in this session about themself (the who).
- Facilitates Client Growth (marker # 3) – Coach invites the client to state or explore the client's learning in this session about their situation (the what).
- Facilitates Client Growth (marker # 4) – Coach invites the client to consider how they will use new learning from this coaching session.

MCC SKILLS[97]

- Establishing Trust and Intimacy – The coach invites the client to share his/her thinking on an equal level with the coach.
- Direct Communication – The coach frequently invites the client's intuition to come forward, and additionally invites, respects, and celebrates direct communication from the client.
- Direct Communication – The coach's communication frequently invites the client to engage in broader learning and discovery and to integrate and apply that learning and discovery not only to present challenges and agendas but also to the creation of the client's future. The coach fully invites the client's participation in the coaching dialogue on an equal level.
- Creating Awareness invites the client to use their greatness, strengths, intuition, and learning style is fully invited and welcomed.
- Creating Awareness – The coach fully invites and allows the client to use as coaching tools the client's intuition, thinking, and learning.

- Creating Awareness – The MCC coach may, as a supplement to client development of tools, suggest tools, exercises, or structures, but invites the client to engage in full thinking about whether these suggestions are of use to the client and invites the client to modify the suggestions, or reject them and invent on their own.
- Designing Actions – The coach invites full client participation in the design of activities.

REMEMBER TO PARTNER AND DO THESE THINGS

- Partnering is evidenced at the very beginning of the coaching relationship during the initial contracting phase when the coach explores what the client wants to accomplish by being coached.
- Partnering continues at the start of each coaching conversation when the coach invites the client to choose where to focus the conversation for that session.
- At the end of the coaching agreement, partnering is evidenced by the coach asking the client where to jump into the topic for the day.
- During the conversation, the client may decide to explore a rabbit trail or to change the topic completely. The coach partners with the client by clarifying the direction in which the client wants to go.
- At some point in the conversation, the coach may offer an observation or insight. The coach partners with the client by inviting the client to respond in any way to the coach's contributions and accepts the client's response.

- In some conversations, the client and coach may do some brainstorming or consider various options for a course of action. The coach partners with the client by playing back the client's various possibilities for the client to choose from.
- Toward the end of the conversation, the coach may choose to partner with the client by encouraging the client to formulate his or her own learning.
- At the conclusion of the conversation, the coach can partner with the client by inquiring if there are other things to be discussed before wrapping up for the conversation to be complete for the client.

SUMMARY

Partnering with the client is an essential skill for masterful coaching. In a coaching conversation, partnering is evidenced by placing the client in a situation to make a choice. Partnering is stressed by the Core Competencies, by the PCC Markers and by the MCC Minimum Skills Required. The more you can partner with a client throughout the coaching conversation, the more you are moving on toward masterful coaching!

SECTION V

Growing in
Your Coaching Skills

24

Guidelines for ICF Credentialing

THE INTERNATIONAL COACHING FEDERATION offers three levels of credentialing.[98]

WHY SEEK A CREDENTIAL?

Two reasons stand out for seeking an ICF credential: credibility and skill development.

Credibility. When you have an ICF credential, others recognize you as a serious coach who has taken training to become a coach. In the corporate world, more and more business executives expect their coach to hold either the PCC or the MCC credential. The ICF holds out the PCC credential as the standard for excellence in coaching. If you hope to serve vocationally as a coach, that is the goal for which you should aim.

Skill development. Each ICF credential requires a higher skill level. Setting your sights on the next higher credential is a good way to motivate yourself toward becoming a better coach with increasingly enhanced coaching skills.

THE DIFFERENCE BETWEEN A CERTIFICATE AND A CREDENTIAL

A coach may be asked, "Are you a certified coach?" or "Are you a credentialed coach?" The two may be easily confused. A certificate is what a coaching school gives to a graduate to indicate that the student has completed the course of study. The coach is certified because they have a certificate. This is similar to achieving a high school diploma or a university degree. One has that diploma or degree for life. A certificate does not necessarily offer proof of a certain skill level.

A credential, on the other hand, is awarded to a coach by an organization to indicate that the individual has achieved a certain level of skill and knowledge. The credential is not permanent but must be renewed. To renew a credential, a coach must take continuing education courses to keep pace with new developments in the field.

THREE PATHWAYS TOWARD A CREDENTIAL

The ICF offers three different pathways in achieving either the ACC or the PCC credential. These are:

1. *Level 1 or Accredited Coach Specific Training Hours (ACSTH) Path.* These schools generally are for students just starting out on their coaching career. Graduates of these schools can apply for the ICF ACC credential. These schools require less of their students, so the ICF has more requirements for applicants using this pathway.
2. *Level 2 or Accredited Coach Training Program (ACTP) Path.* These schools usually have both beginning level courses for students just starting out and intermediate

level courses for those who have been coaching for a while. Graduates of the latter course can apply for the ICF PCC credential. Because these schools require more of their students, the ICF has fewer requirements for applicants using this pathway.

3. *Portfolio Path.* Those applying using this pathway likely have not completed a course from an ICF accredited coaching school. Perhaps they have completed a course from a non-approved school, or perhaps they have taken various seminars to accumulate the needed sixty coach specific training hours or continuing education (CCE) hours. The ICF has the most requirements of students using this pathway.

REQUIREMENTS FOR THE ACC CREDENTIAL

	LEVEL 2/ ACTP Path	Level 1/ ACSTH Path	Portfolio Path
Coach Specific Training	60 hours	60 hours	60 hours
Mentor-Coaching		10 hours	10 hours
Coaching Log	100 hours	100 hours	100 hours
Pass Credentialing Exam	Yes	Yes	Yes
One Recording & Transcript		Yes	Yes

REQUIREMENTS FOR THE PCC CREDENTIAL

	Level 2/ ACTP Path	Level 1/ ACSTH Path	Portfolio Path
Coach-Specific Training	125 hours	125 hours	125 hours
Mentor-Coaching		10 hours	10 hours
Coaching Log	500 hours	500 hours	500 hours
Pass Credentialing Exam	Yes	Yes	Yes
Two Recordings & Transcripts		Yes	Yes

REQUIREMENTS FOR THE MCC CREDENTIAL

	Level 3 Path	Portfolio Path
Coach-Specific Training	200 hours	200 hours
Mentor-Coaching		10 hours
Coaching Log	2,500 hours	2,500 hours
Pass Credentialing Exam	Yes	Yes
Two Recordings & Transcripts	Yes	Yes

SUMMARY

The ICF offers three levels of credentialing: ACC, PCC, and MCC. Motivations for seeking an ICF credential include credibility and skill development. There are three paths to an ICF credential: Level 1 or ACSTH, Level 2 or ACTP, and Portfolio. Each pathway has different requirements for obtaining the ACC and PCC credential, while MCC applicants use either Level 3 path or the portfolio path.

25

Becoming a Masterful Coach

COACHING IS BOTH A skill and an art. Like other things that require extensive skill, coaching takes time to learn. Journalist Malcom Gladwell popularized the idea that to become an expert in something, one must invest about ten thousand hours in that endeavor.[99] Here are some suggestions to shorten the learning curve toward becoming an effective coach.

COACH A LOT

One of the best ways to learn any skill is to practice. To become a masterful coach requires coaching a great deal. To apply for the MCC (Master Certified Coach) with the ICF, a coach must provide a coaching log demonstrating at least twenty-five hundred hours of coaching.

One marketing class put on by Coach U, the largest coaching school in the world, requires that students have one hundred clients to complete the course. They suggest that you ask everyone you meet to let you coach them. Using this approach, a new coach could accumulate several hundred coaching hours in just a few months.

READ GOOD BOOKS ON COACHING

Reading some of the best books about coaching skills will help you become a better coach. These books will provide a mental framework to grasp what coaching is all about. Reading and applying what you learn will move you forward more quickly. Some of the best I have found (listed alphabetically) are:

- *Co-Active Coaching* by Laura Whitworth, Henry Kimsey-House, Karem Kimsey-House, and Phillip Sandahl
- *Coaching for Performance* by John Whitmore
- *Executive Coaching with Backbone and Heart* by Mary Beth O'Neill
- *Handbook of Coaching* by Pamela McLean
- *Professional Coach Training* by Val Hastings
- *The Coaching Manual* by Julie Starr
- *The Extraordinary Coach* by John Zenger and Kathleen Stinnett
- *TransforMissional Coaching* by Steve Ogne and Tim Roehl

TAKE A COACHING COURSE

Today there are hundreds of coaching schools eager to help you learn coaching skills. The ICF has recognized many of these schools as being either approved or accredited. Some schools are recognized as ACSTH (approved coach-specific training hours) that can equip students to apply for the ACC credential with sixty hours of teaching. Other schools are recognized as ACTP (accredited coach training program) that can prepare students to apply for the PCC credential with 125 hours of teaching.

JOIN THE ICF AND BECOME ACTIVE IN A LOCAL CHAPTER

If you are serious about becoming a professional coach, consider membership in the International Coach Federation. ICF membership offers many benefits, one of which is becoming active in a local chapter where you can meet other coaches. In addition to their monthly meetings with guest speakers, ICF chapters often offer webinars and conferences where beginning coaches can learn and sharpen their skills.

LEARN THE PCC MARKERS

The thirty-two PCC markers summarize the behaviors or skills expected of a professional coach. Learning these markers and understanding the behavior each marker calls for will help the coach immensely in comprehending what it takes to become a truly good coach.

LISTEN TO YOUR RECORDINGS

Here is something that will speed up acquiring coaching skills for you. Frequently record a coaching session and listen to it, using the PCC markers as a guideline for determining your skill level. (Note: you must get the client's permission to record the session. Failure to do so would be violating confidentiality expected in the ICF Code of Ethics, Section Four.)

When I applied the first time for the PCC credential, I was turned down. I had not even heard of the PCC markers at the time. Soon after, I learned that these markers were the determining factors by which an applicant was judged. I got a copy and memorized the forty-seven (original) markers. I then created a checklist by which I could evaluate a coaching session. I committed to recording a coaching conversation once a week and evaluating it according to the PCC markers. The first time I did so, I was able to check only twenty-three markers, but nine months later, I was consistently demonstrating about forty-two or forty-three of the skills. When I applied again for the PCC credential, this time I easily passed! Without question, listening to my own recordings has been the best tool for growing my coaching skills.

HIRE A MENTOR COACH

The ICF requires at least ten hours of mentor coaching in order to apply for one of its credentials. While you will get more attention from one-on-one sessions, up to seven hours may be obtained from group coaching in a class setting.

A mentor coach may be anyone who has an ICF credential at a higher level than the one you hold. There are courses a coach can take to become a certified mentor coach (the CMC credential). You may want to find a mentor coach who is also an ICF assessor. Assessors listen to recordings from ICF credential applicants and help determine whether they are coaching at that specific credential level. You would be assured of having the best if you can find a mentor coach who holds the Certified Mentor Coach (CMC) credential, who has experience as a mentor coach, and who also is an ICF assessor. (You can expect to pay several hundred dollars an hour when working with this kind of an experienced mentor coach.)

A mentor coach listens to several of your coach recordings and reads transcripts of them and should provide verbal feedback on some recordings and written feedback on others. The mentor coach would expect you to take their feedback seriously and incorporate their suggestions into your coaching.

BECOME A MENTOR COACH YOURSELF

A good way to sharpen your coaching skills and become a masterful coach is to become a mentor coach yourself. In listening to dozens of coaching conversations and providing feedback, your awareness of what constitutes excellent coaching is significantly enhanced.

EVEN BEGINNING COACHES HELP SIGNIFICANTLY

Please do not let this discussion of becoming a masterful coach deter you from even starting on your coaching journey! Remember, even beginning coaches can help another person significantly by listening well and asking good questions. Be patient with yourself, give yourself time, and with practice you can grow to become a very fine coach.

SUMMARY

Coaching is a skill and an art that takes time to develop. Like many other things, practice makes perfect. These suggestions will shorten your journey to becoming a masterful coach: coach a great deal, read good books on coaching, take a coaching course, join the ICF and a local chapter, memorize the PCC markers, evaluate your own coach recordings, hire a mentor coach, and become a mentor coach yourself.

By pursuing coaching skills, you can help transform the lives of many people!

HAPPY COACHING!

26

What Is Christian Coaching?

CHRISTIAN COACHING IS A non-directive intentional conversation in which a person of faith partners with another person of faith to help them gain clarity or new perspectives. Ideally, the person successfully moves toward their God-inspired goals, while achieving personal and professional growth.

Christian coaches use many of the same communication and coaching tools that non-Christian coaches use. The key difference is in their worldview, their beliefs, and their reliance upon the Holy Spirit to offer guidance and insights. At the heart of Christian coaching is the client's awareness of where God is leading the client. Conversations that include a focus on faith and spirituality can be important topics in the coaching relationship.

A Christian coach utilizes professional coaching skills to empower clients to change, to create new awareness, and move forward, while not losing sight of the bigger picture of the human condition that is informed by a biblical worldview.

DEFINITIONS BY CCNI

Christian Coaches Network International, an organization that provides support for Christian coaches, has adopted the following definitions.

Christian coaching is an approach to the practice of professional coaching—whether focused on personal or professional growth—that integrates the biblical worldview when working with clients to recognize their potential and effect personal change. Whereas the biblical worldview is given priority over existing theories of human nature, motivation, personal change, growth and development as well as frame the perspectives by which coaching is offered.

Christian coaching is a professional relationship focused on empowering a person or group to effect change, create new awareness, move into action and step into abundant Christian life in business and in personal areas.[100]

CHRISTIAN COACHES HAVE AN ADVANTAGE

A Christian coach has an advantage over a non-Christian coach in several ways, including supportive beliefs and the presence of the Holy Spirit. A Christian belief system and a biblical worldview greatly influence a coach's attitudes and behaviors toward clients.

- The Christian coach believes that God seeks active involvement in the lives of each human being. God has a plan for each individual. An important aspect of Christian coaching is assisting the client in discerning and following that plan.
- The Christian coach knows that God loves and highly values each person. Every individual is of infinite worth and significance. This realty is reflected in how the coach relates to the client.

- The Christian coach acknowledges the fallen state of humanity, and that each person is in need of a Savior. Through faith in Jesus Christ the broken relationship with their Creator can be restored.
- The Christian coach knows that reconciliation with God is necessary for a person to reach their God-given potential. Knowing God in an intimate personal relationship is the greatest good that can happen to anyone.
- The Christian coach sees that coming into a relationship with Jesus initiates an inward transformation process that transforms inward thought processes and outward behaviors.
- The Christian coach adheres to an eternal perspective that shapes attitudes and choices in the present life. This eternal perspective greatly influences core values and everyday decisions.
- The Christian coach fosters hope for positive change in a client not just in coaching techniques but in the belief that God is at work in the client's life and that God desires the best for that person.
- The Christian coach realizes that God has been at work in the client's life long before the coach came on the scene. The coach's best approach in working with the client is to discover what God is doing in that person's life and to partner with God in that effort.

THE ROLE OF THE HOLY SPIRIT IN COACHING

- The Holy Spirit is the Third Person of the Trinity—Father, Son, and Spirit. The Holy Spirit is co-equal with the Father and with Jesus. The Holy Spirit is a

Person, having emotions, intellect, and will. The Holy Spirit indwells every believer.

- The Holy Spirit is the Advocate, the Comforter, the Paraclete—the One who comes alongside to help (John 14:16–17).
- The Holy Spirit brings conviction of sin and causes the unbeliever to see the truth of the gospel (John 16:8–11).
- The Holy Spirit unites us with Christ and places us into the Body of Christ, the Church (1 Corinthians 12:13; Romans 6:3–5).
- The Holy Spirit is the Teacher Who guides into all truth (John 14:26; 16:13).
- The Holy Spirit testifies of Jesus and reminds us of Jesus' teachings (John 14:26; 15:26).
- The Holy Spirit empowers believers to live a victorious life and produces the fruit of the Spirit within them (Acts 1:8; Galatians 5:16, 22–23).
- The Holy Spirit bestows spiritual gifts or special abilities for serving (Romans 12:3–8).

THE HOLY SPIRIT AS COACH

In a sense, the Holy Spirit serves as the Coach for every believer. An appropriate mindset for the Christian coach is to recognize the Spirit's coaching role in clients and to consider oneself as a junior coach or coaching apprentice to the Holy Spirit. In this sense, the Christian coach should take seriously the responsibility to listen to the Holy Spirit on behalf of each client, and to consider oneself as the junior partner in this three-way coaching relationship.

The Holy Spirit "coaches" people in many ways. The Spirit is the best resource for new insights, ideas, strategies, and action steps. The Christian coach will help clients to hear the Holy Spirit and encourage them to respond positively.

CHRISTIAN COACHES AND THE ICF CORE COMPETENCIES

Christian coaches are well equipped through biblical teachings and tenants of the faith to adhere to the core competencies of the ICF.

DEMONSTRATES ETHICAL PRACTICE

A great deal of the Code of Ethics has to do with honesty, non-discrimination, keeping confidences and relating to others in appropriate ways. The Christian coach adheres to the Golden Rule: *Do to others what you would have them do to you* (Mathew 7:12). Numerous passages from the Bible teach honesty. Four commands from the Ten Commandments include:

> You shall not murder.
> You shall not commit adultery.
> You shall not steal.
> You shall not give false testimony against your
> neighbor. (Exodus 20:13–16)

These verses insist on honesty for all Christians.

- "We are taking pains to do what is right, not only in the eyes of the Lord but also in the eyes of man" (2 Corinthians 8:21).
- "Do not lie to each other, since you have taken off your old self with its practices" (Colossians 3:9).

- "Each of you must put off falsehood and speak truthfully to your neighbor" (Ephesians 4:25).
- "Whoever walks in integrity walks securely, but whoever takes crooked paths will be found out" (Proverbs 10:9)
- "The LORD detests lying lips, but he delights in people who are trustworthy" (Proverbs 12:22).
- "Whoever would love life and see good days must keep their tongue from evil and their lips from deceitful speech" (1 Peter 3:10).
- "A gossip betrays a confidence, but a trustworthy person keeps a secret" (Proverbs 11:13).

ESTABLISHES AND MAINTAINS AGREEMENTS

The coaching agreement has to do both with the initial contracting for the coaching relationship and with the outcome goal for each individual coaching conversation. The coaching agreement sets the stage for healthy relationships, as well as for setting goals and strategizing to reach those goals. Christian teachings support healthy relationships and planning for a preferred future.

Christian coaches are instructed to put a high priority on healthy relationships in these Bible verses.

- "An expert in the law tested Jesus with this question: 'Teacher, which is the greatest commandment in the Law?' Jesus replied: ' "Love the Lord your God with all your heart and with all your soul and with all your mind." ' This is the first and greatest commandment. And the second is like it: "Love your neighbor as yourself" ' " (Matthew 22:35–39).

- "If you are offering your gift at the altar and there remember that your brother or sister has something against you, leave your gift there in front of the altar. First go and be reconciled to them; then come and offer your gift" (Matthew 5:23-24).
- "If your brother or sister sins against you, go and point out their fault, just between the two of you. If they listen to you, you have won them over" (Matthew 18:15).
- "Do nothing out of selfish ambition or vain conceit. Rather, in humility value others above yourselves, not looking to your own interests but each of you to the interests of the others" (Philippians 2:3–4).
- "Do not repay anyone evil for evil. Be careful to do what is right in the eyes of everyone. If it is possible, as far as it depends on you, live at peace with everyone" (Romans 12:17–18).
- "Above all, love each other deeply, because love covers over a multitude of sins" (1 Peter 4:8).

Christian coaches have learned from the Bible that goal setting and planning is necessary.

- "Therefore, everyone who hears these words of mine and puts them into practice is like a wise man who built his house on the rock. The rain came down, the streams rose, and the winds blew and beat against that house; yet it did not fall, because it had its foundation on the rock. But everyone who hears these words of mine and does not put them into practice is like a foolish man who built his house on sand. The rain came down, the streams rose, and the winds blew and beat against that house, and it fell with a great crash" (Matthew 7:24–27).

- "Suppose a king is about to go to war against another king. Won't he first sit down and consider whether he is able with ten thousand men to oppose the one coming against him with twenty thousand?" (Luke 14:31)
- "Suppose one of you wants to build a tower. Won't you first sit down and estimate the cost to see if you have enough money to complete it?" (Luke 14:28)
- "May He give you the desire of your heart and make all your plans succeed" (Psalm 20:4).
- "Teach us to number our days, that we may gain a heart of wisdom" (Psalm 90:12).
- "Commit to the LORD whatever you do, and he will establish your plans" (Proverbs 16:3).

CULTIVATES TRUST AND SAFETY

Trust is the foundation for an effective coaching relationship. Trust is established with a client over time as the coach is consistent in relating, as the coach listens with obvious interest without interrupting, and as the coach unfailingly demonstrates having the client's best interest in mind. The Christian coach knows the importance of these things through numerous Bible teachings.

- "Let your 'Yes' be 'Yes,' and your 'No,' 'No' " (Matthew 5:37 nkjv).
- "Be completely humble and gentle; be patient, bearing with one another in love. Make every effort to keep the unity of the Spirit through the bond of peace" (Ephesians 4:2–3).

- "I try to please everyone in every way. For I am not seeking my own good but the good of many" (1 Corinthians 10:33).
- "Be devoted to one another in love. Honor one another above yourselves" (Romans 12:10).
- "Do to others as you would have them do to you" (Luke 6:31).
- "Be kind and compassionate to one another, forgiving each other, just as in Christ God forgave you" (Ephesians 4:32).
- "My command is this: Love each other as I have loved you" (John 15:12).
- "Above all, love each other deeply, because love covers over a multitude of sins" (1 Peter 4:8).
- "It is right for me to feel this way about all of you, since I have you in my heart" (Philippians 1:7).
- "Now that you have purified yourselves by obeying the truth so that you have sincere love for each other, love one another deeply, from the heart" (1 Peter 1:22).

MAINTAINS PRESENCE

Coaching presence implies being 100 percent focused on the other person. The Christian coach is familiar with the concept of focusing completely on Christ in times of prayer and worship, so it is easy to transfer that complete focus onto the client.

- Fix your thoughts on Jesus, whom we acknowledge as our apostle and high priest (Hebrews 3:1).
- Set your minds on things above, not on earthly things (Colossians 3:2).

LISTENS ACTIVELY

Christian coaches know well the importance of deep listening while withholding judgment, based upon the teachings of the Bible.

- "My dear brothers and sisters, take note of this: Everyone should be quick to listen, slow to speak and slow to become angry" (James 1:19).
- "To answer before listening—that is folly and shame" (Proverbs 18:13).
- "The way of fools seems right to them, but the wise listen" (Proverbs 12:15).
- "Fools find no pleasure in understanding, but delight in airing their own opinions" (Proverbs 18:2).
- "Turn your heart to wisdom and apply your heart to understanding" (Proverbs 2:2).
- "There is a time for everything . . . a time to be silent and a time to speak" (Ecclesiastes 3:1,7).
- "Do not judge, or you too will be judged" (Matthew 7:1).

EVOKES AWARENESS

Evoking awareness is about aiding clients in gaining new perspectives, insights, and understanding. The Bible places a high value on gaining knowledge and understanding.

- "My son, if you accept my words and store up my commands within you, turning your ear to wisdom and applying your heart to understanding—indeed, if you call out for insight and cry aloud for understanding, and if you look for it as for silver and search

for it as for hidden treasure, then you will understand
... and find knowledge" (Proverbs 2:1–5).

- "Blessed are those who find wisdom, those who gain understanding, for she is more profitable than silver and yields better returns than gold. She is more precious than rubies; nothing you desire can compare with her" (Proverbs 3:13–15).
- "The beginning of wisdom is this: Get wisdom. Though it cost all you have, get understanding" (Proverbs 4:7).
- "Reflect on what I am saying, for the LORD will give you insight into all this" (2 Timothy 2:7).
- "The fear of the LORD is the beginning of wisdom; all who follow his precepts have good understanding" (Psalm 111:10).
- "If any of you lacks wisdom, you should ask God, who gives generously to all without finding fault, and it will be given to you" (James 1:5).
- "The Advocate, the Holy Spirit, whom the Father will send in my name, will teach you all things and will remind you of everything I have said to you . . . When he, the Spirit of truth, comes, he will guide you into all the truth" (John 14:26; 16:13).

POWERFUL QUESTIONING

The ability to ask powerful questions is a key skill for the Christian coach. In doing so they follow the example of Jesus, who was a master at asking questions. Jesus frequently used questions to create change and growth. The four Gospels record 307 questions that Jesus asked, including:

- "What do you want?" (John 1:38)
- "What do you want me to do for you?" (Matt 20:32)

- "What profit would there be for one to gain the whole world and forfeit his life?" (Matthew 16:26)
- "What can one give in exchange for their soul?" (Matthew 16:26)
- "What did Moses command you?" (Mark 10:3)
- "Why are you thinking these things in your hearts?" (Luke 5:22)
- "Where is your faith?" (Luke 8:25)
- "What is that to you?" (John 21:22)

Christianity teaches its followers to probe intensely for answers to life's deepest questions. Jesus commended the use of questions when searching for truth when He said, "Ask and it will be given to you. Seek and you will find . . . For everyone who asks receives; the one who seeks finds" (Matthew 7:7-8). Christianity began a whole new era when Peter answered the questions the crowd was asking: "How is it that each of us hears them in our native language? We hear them declaring the wonders of God in our own tongues!" Amazed and perplexed, they asked one another, "What does this mean?" (Acts 2:8, 11–12).

Christianity is not afraid of deep questions. Christian philosophers have debated the most difficult questions, including:

- What lies beyond the observable universe?
- What came before the big bang?
- Are there more than three dimensions?
- How did life on earth evolve?
- Is there life after death?
- What is the nature of reality?
- Is there something greater than ourselves?

DIRECT COMMUNICATION

While beginning coaches do well to use direct communication sparingly, masterful Christian coaches use it frequently and effectively. The Bible gives clear instructions on saying things directly to others.

- "A word fitly spoken is like apples of gold in pictures of silver" (Proverbs 25:11 NKJV).
- "Speaking the truth in love, we will grow" (Ephesians 4:15).
- "Each of you must put off falsehood and speak truthfully to your neighbor" (Ephesians 4:25).
- "Do not let any unwholesome talk come out of your mouths, but only what is helpful for building others up according to their needs, that it may benefit those who listen" (Ephesians 4:29).
- "When words are many, transgression is not lacking, but whoever restrains his lips is prudent" (Proverbs 10:19 ESV).
- "The one who has knowledge uses words with restraint" (Proverbs 17:27).
- "A gentle answer turns away wrath, but a harsh word stirs up anger" (Proverbs 15:1).
- "If I speak in the tongues of men or of angels, but do not have love, I am only a resounding gong or a clanging cymbal" (1 Corinthians 13:1).

DESIGNING ACTIONS

Action steps provide the way for a client to move forward. Christian coaches assist clients in designing appropriate actions, keeping in mind biblical teaching on taking actions.

- "The steps of a good man are ordered by the LORD: and he delights in his way" (Psalm 37:23 NKJV).
- "Now listen, you who say, 'Today or tomorrow we will go to this or that city, spend a year there, carry on business and make money.' Why, you do not even know what will happen tomorrow. What is your life? You are a mist that appears for a little while and then vanishes. Instead, you ought to say, 'If it is the Lord's will, we will live and do this or that.' " (James 4:13–15).

PLANNING AND GOAL SETTING

God is a planner. He designed a plan for creation and for this universe. He designed a plan for the salvation of humanity. God has a plan for each person: " 'For I know the plans I have for you,' declares the LORD, 'plans to prosper you and not to harm you, plans to give you hope and a future' " (Jeremiah 29:11).

The Christian coach also must be a planner in designing a coaching plan for clients to help them reach their goals. The coach relies not only on the client to give direction for these plans, but also upon the Holy Spirit's guidance.

- "Many are the plans in a person's heart, but it is the LORD's purpose that prevails" (Proverbs 19:21).
- "In their hearts humans plan their course, but the LORD establishes their steps" (Proverbs 16:9).
- "Seek first his kingdom and his righteousness, and all these things will be given to you as well" (Matthew 6:33).
- "In all your ways submit to him, and he will make your paths straight" (Proverbs 3:6).

MANAGING PROGRESS AND ACCOUNTABILITY

Managing progress and accountability is the ability to focus attention on what is important for the client, but to leave responsibility with the client. The Christian coach keeps in mind biblical exhortations in order to do this well.

- "Encourage one another and build each other up, just as in fact you are doing" (1 Thessalonians 5:11).
- "Where there is no guidance, a people falls" (Proverbs 11:14 ESV).
- "Be very careful, then, how you live—not as unwise but as wise, making the most of every opportunity, because the days are evil. Therefore, do not be foolish, but understand what the Lord's will is" (Ephesians 5:15–17).
- "Walk in wisdom . . . making the best use of the time" (Colossians 4:5 ESV).
- "Be shepherds of God's flock that is under your care, watching over them—not because you must, but because you are willing, as God wants you to be; not pursuing dishonest gain, but eager to serve; not lording it over those entrusted to you, but being examples to the flock" (1 Peter 5:2–3).

PARTNERING

The scriptures teach the value of partnership.

- "Two are better than one, because they have a good return for their labor" (Ecclesiastes 4:9).

- "Though one may be overpowered, two can defend themselves. A cord of three strands is not quickly broken" (Ecclesiastes 4:12).
- "Do two walk together unless they have agreed to do so?" (Amos 3:3)
- "As iron sharpens iron, so one person sharpens another" (Proverbs 27:17).
- "I always pray with joy because of your partnership" (Philippians 1:4).

SUMMARY

While Christian coaches use many of the same communication and coaching tools that non-Christian coaches use, there is a significant difference in what they bring to a coaching relationship. These differences include their worldview, their beliefs, and their reliance upon the Holy Spirit to provide guidance and insights.

My point of view is that Christian coaches have an advantage over non-Christian coaches because of their faith and beliefs, as well as their reliance upon the Holy Spirit. Christian beliefs harmonize well with the core competencies of the ICF and give the Christian coach a head start in acquiring masterful coaching skills.

Notes

Chapter One: What Is Coaching?
[1] ICF. "All Things Coaching," About Page, accessed October 26, 2023, www.coachfederation.org/about.
[2] J. Val Hastings, *Professional Coach Training: Developing Ministry Excellence and Effectiveness* (Harrisburg, Pa.: Coaching4Clergy, 2011), 2-3.
[3] Keith E. Webb, *The Coaching Workshop* (Bellevue, Wa.: Active Results, 2013), 21.
[4] Hastings, *Professional Coach Training*, 5.
[5] "Introduction to Coaching" workshop, Portland, New Hampshire, June 13, 2000.

Chapter Two: Overview of the CHRISP Coaching Model
[6] Peter Hawkins, https://www.personal-coaching-information.com/clear-coaching-model.html, accessed November 19, 2023.
[7] Sir John Whitmore, *Coaching for Performance,* Third Edition (Nicholas Brealey Publishing, 2002), 54.
[8] Robert E. Logan and Sherilyn Carlton, *Coaching 101* (St. Charles, Ill.: ChurchSmart Resources, 2003) 29.
[9] Coach U, *Personal and Corporate Coach Training Handbook* (New York: John Wiley & Sons, 2005).
[10] Keith E. Webb, *The COACH Model for Christian Leaders* (New York: Morgan James Publishing, 2019).
[11] "Chrisp" by louloulovespink, February 22, 2012, https://www.urbandictionary.com/define.php?term=Chrisp.

Chapter Three: Phase 1: C = Connect
[12] ICF Core Competencies, www.coachfederation.org/core-competencies, accessed November 8, 2023.
[13] *New Webster's Dictionary* (New York: Book Essentials, Inc., 1991), 89.
[14] S. John Powell, *Why Am I Afraid to Tell You Who I Am?* (Grand Rapids: Zondervan, 1999).
[15] Related in a Coach U Advanced Coaching Course, 2016.

Chapter Four: Phase 2: H = Homework
[16] ICF Core Competencies, www.coachfederation.org/core-competencies, accessed November 8, 2023.

Chapter Five: Phase 3: R = Result
[17] ICF Core Competencies, www.coachfederation.org/core-competencies, accessed November 8, 2023.

Chapter Six: Phase 4: I = Investigate
[18] ICF Core Competencies, www.coachfederation.org/core-competencies, April 26, 2023,
[19] Michael Marquardt, *Leading with Questions: How Leaders Find the Right Solutions by Knowing What to Ask* (San Francisco: Jossey-Bass, a Wiley Imprint, 2005), 141.

Chapter Seven: Phase 5: S = Steps
[20] ICF Core Competencies, www.coachfederation.org/core-competencies, accessed November 8, 2023.
[21] Keith Webb, "How to Get People into Action with One Simple Question," *Multiply Your Impact* blog, https://keithwebb.com/how-to-get-people-into-action-with-one-simple-question/.

Chapter Eight: Phase 6: P = Purpose
[22] ICF Core Competencies, www.coachfederation.org/core-competencies, accessed November 8, 2019.

Chapter Nine: Overview of the ICF Core Competencies
[23] Global Coaching Study Executive Summary, https://coachingfederation.org/app/uploads/2023/04/2023ICFGlobalCoachingStudy ExecutiveSummary.pdf, August 14, 2023.
[24] ICF Credentialing, www.coachfeeration.org/icf-credential, accessed November 8, 2023.
[25] ICF Competencies, https://coachingfederation.org/credentials-and-standards/core-competencies, August 30, 2023
[26] ICF Credentialing, https://coachingfederation.org/credentials-and-standards/credentials-paths, August 30, 2023.

Chapter Ten: Demonstrates Ethical Practice
[27] ICF Code of Ethics, www.coachfederation.org/code-of-ethics, accessed November 9, 2023.

[28] ICF Minimum Skill Requirements for ACC Credential, https://coachingfederation.org/credentials-and-standards/performance-evaluations/minimum-skills-requirements, accessed November 9, 2023.
[29] Ibid.
[30] Ibid.
[31] ICF Ethical Standards, https://coachingfederation.org/ethics/code-of-ethics, September 1, 2023.
[32] "Updated ICF Core Competency 1: Demonstrates Ethical Practice," YouTube, December 7, 2020, https://www.youtube.com/watch?v=7pxYhGVI2h0&list=PLMBtOVpaN5DjRt-VAJIa0Xe0M-LuA-LZNk.
[33] Suggested by Dr. Michael Marx, Core Competencies Education Group, ICF Colorado Chapter, February 28, 2020.

Chapter Eleven: Embodies a Coaching Mindset
[34] ICF Core Competencies, https://coachingfederation.org/credentials-and-standards/core-competencies, April 26, 2023.
[35] PCC Markers, www.coachfederation.org/pcc-markers, November 19, 2020.
[36] ICF PCC Markers, https://coachingfederation.org/credentials-and-standards/performance-evaluations/pcc-markers, April 26, 2023.

Chapter Twelve: Establishes and Maintains Agreements
[37] ICF Core Competencies, www.coachfederation.org/core-competencies, accessed November 19, 2023.
[38] Ibid.
[39] ICF Minimum Skill Requirements, https://coachingfederation.org/credentials-and-standards/performance-evaluations/minimum-skills-requirements, September 1, 2023.
[40] Summarized from "Resource Guide for Core Competencies" (ICF document, PCC Markers Training, 2016).

Chapter Thirteen: Cultivates Trust and Safety
[41] ICF Core Competencies, https://coachingfederation.org/credentials-and-standards/core-competencies, April 26, 2023.
[42] Minimum Skills Requirements, https://coachingfederation.org/credentials-and-standards/performance-evaluations/minimum-skills-requirements, July 28, 2023.
[43] PCC Markers, https://coachingfederation.org/credentials-and-standards/performance-evaluations/pcc-markers, April 26, 2023.

44 Minimum Skills Requirements, https://coachingfederation.org/credentials-and-standards/performance-evaluations/minimum-skills-requirements, July 28, 2023.
45 Summarized from "Resource Guide for Core Competencies" (ICF document, PCC Markers Training, 2016).

Chapter Fourteen: Maintains Presence
46 ICF Core Competencies, https://coachingfederation.org/credentials-and-standards/core-competencies, April 21, 2023.
47 Minimum Skills Requirements, https://coachingfederation.org/credentials-and-standards/performance-evaluations/minimum-skills-requirements, July 28, 2023.
48 PCC Markers, https://coachingfederation.org/credentials-and-standards/performance-evaluations/pcc-markers, April 3, 2023.
49 Minimum Skills Requirements, https://coachingfederation.org/credentials-and-standards/performance-evaluations/minimum-skills-requirements, July 28, 2023.
50 Summarized from "Resource Guide for Core Competencies" (ICF document, PCC Markers Training, 2016).

Chapter Fifteen: Listens Actively
51 ICF Core Competencies, https://coachingfederation.org/credentials-and-standards/performance-evaluations/minimum-skills-requirements, July 14, 2023.
52 Minimum Skill Requirements at the ACC Level, https://coachingfederation.org/credentials-and-standards/performance-evaluations/minimum-skills-requirements, July 13, 2023.
53 PCC Markers, https://coachingfederation.org/credentials-and-standards/performance-evaluations/pcc-markers, April 3, 2023.
54 ICF Core Competencies, https://coachingfederation.org/credentials-and-standards/performance-evaluations/minimum-skills-requirements, July 14, 2023.
55 Minimum Skill Requirements at the MCC Level, https://coachingfederation.org/credentials-and-standards/performance-evaluations/minimum-skills-requirements, July 13, 2023.
56 Derber, Charles (2000). *The pursuit of attention: power and ego in everyday life.* Oxford University Press
57 Jack Zenger and Joseph Folkman, "What Great Listeners Actually Do" (https://hbr.org/2016/07/what-great-listeners-actually-do?, Harvard Business Review, July 14, 2016), November 9. 2019.

[58] Summarized from "Resource Guide for Core Competencies" (ICF document, PCC Markers Training, 2016).

Chapter Sixteen: Evokes Awareness
[59] ICF Core Competencies, https://coachingfederation.org/credentials-and-standards/core-competencies, May 21, 2023.
[60] Minimum Skills Requirements, https://coachingfederation.org/credentials-and-standards/performance-evaluations/minimum-skills-requirements, July 28, 2023.
[61] Updated PCC Markers, https://coachingfederation.org/app/uploads/2020/11/Updated-PCC-Markers_November-2020.pdf, July28, 2023
[62] Minimum Skills Requirements, https://coachingfederation.org/credentials-and-standards/performance-evaluations/minimum-skills-requirements, July 28, 2023.
[63] Summarized from "Resource Guide for Core Competencies" (ICF document, PCC Markers Training, 2016).

Chapter 17: Facilitates Client Growth
[64] ICF Core Competencies, https://coachingfederation.org/credentials-and-standards/core-competencies, May 21, 2023.
[65] "ICF Core Competencies Ratings Levels", adapted from "Minimum Skills Requirements" document (www.coachfederation.org/msr, 2006), November 9, 2019.
[66] Minimum Skills Requirements, https://coachingfederation.org/credentials-and-standards/performance-evaluations/minimum-skills-requirements, July 28, 2023.
[67] PCC Markers, https://coachingfederation.org/credentials-and-standards/performance-evaluations/pcc-markers, May 23, 2023.
[68] Minimum Skills Requirements, https://coachingfederation.org/credentials-and-standards/performance-evaluations/minimum-skills-requirements, July 28, 2023.

Chapter Eighteen: Powerful Questioning
[69] "ICF Core Competencies Ratings Levels", adapted from "Minimum Skills Requirements" document (www.coachfederation.org/msr, 2006), November 9, 2019.
[70] PCC Markers, www.coachfederation.org/pcc-markers, November 9, 2019.
[71] Summarized from "Resource Guide for Core Competencies" (ICF document, PCC Markers Training, 2016).

Chapter Nineteen: Direct Communication

[72] ICF Core Competencies, www.coachfederation.org/core-competencies, November 8, 2019.

[73] Ibid.

[74] "ICF Core Competencies Ratings Levels", adapted from "Minimum Skills Requirements" document (www.coachfederation.org/msr, 2006), November 9, 2019.

[75] PCC Markers, www.coachfederation.org/pcc-markers, November 9, 2019.

[76] Stated by Keith Webb in a Train-the-Trainer course, Seattle, 2012.

[77] Summarized from "Resource Guide for Core Competencies" (ICF document, PCC Markers Training, 2016).

Chapter Twenty: Designing Actions

[78] ICF Core Competencies, www.coachfederation.org/core-competencies, November 8, 2019.

[79] "ICF Core Competencies Ratings Levels", adapted from "Minimum Skills Requirements" document (www.coachfederation.org/msr, 2006), November 9, 2019.

[80] PCC Markers, www.coachfederation.org/pcc-markers, November 9, 2019

[81] Summarized from "Resource Guide for Core Competencies" (ICF document, PCC Markers Training, 2016).

Chapter Twenty-One: Planning and Goal Setting

[82] ICF Core Competencies, www.coachfederation.org/core-competencies, November 8, 2019.

[83] "ICF Core Competencies Ratings Levels", adapted from "Minimum Skills Requirements" document (www.coachfederation.org/msr, 2006), November 9, 2019.

[84] PCC Markers, www.coachfederation.org/pcc-markers, November 9, 2019

[85] Summarized from "Resource Guide for Core Competencies" (ICF document, PCC Markers Training, 2016).

Chapter Twenty-Two: Managing Progress and Accountability

[86] ICF Core Competencies, www.coachfederation.org/core-competencies, November 8, 2019.

[87] Ibid.

[88] "ICF Core Competencies Ratings Levels", adapted from "Minimum Skills Requirements" document (www.coachfederation.org/msr, 2006), November 9, 2019.

[89] PCC Markers, www.coachfederation.org/pcc-markers, November 9, 2019

[90] Summarized from "Resource Guide for Core Competencies" (ICF document, PCC Markers Training, 2016).

Chapter Twenty-Three: Partnering with Clients

[91] ICF – What is Coaching? https://coachingfederation.org/about, September 2, 2023.

[92] J. Val Hastings, *Professional Coach Training: Developing Ministry Excellence and Effectiveness* (Coaching4Clergy, 2011), 2-3.

[93] Merriam-Webster Dictionary, https://www.merriam-webster.com/dictionary/partner, September 2, 2023.

[94] Giuseppe Totino, stated in Essence of Mastery Summit, May 20, 2022.

[95] ICF Core Competencies, https://coachingfederation.org/credentials-and-standards/core-competencies, September 2, 2023.

[96] ICF PCC Markers, https://coachingfederation.org/credentials-and-standards/performance-evaluations/pcc-markers, September 2, 2023.

[97] ICF Minimum Skills Requirements, https://coachingfederation.org/credentials-and-standards/performance-evaluations/minimum-skills-requirements, September 2, 2023.

Chapter Twenty-Four: Guidelines for ICF Credentialing

[98] ICF Credential, https://coachingfederation.org/credentials-and-standards/credentials-paths

Chapter Twenty-Five: Becoming a Masterful Coach

[99] Malcolm Gladwell, *Outliers* (New York: Little, Brown & Company, 2008).

Chapter Twenty-Six: What Is Christian Coaching?

[100] Christian Coaches Network, International, https://christian-coaches.com/wp-content/uploads/2017/10/CCNI-Christian-Coaching-Distinctions.pdf, August 8, 2020.

About the Author

DR. WALT HASTINGS HAS been coaching for twenty-five years. He has earned the master certified coach (MCC) credential, the highest skill level recognized by the International Coaching Federation (ICF). He also holds the doctor of ministry (DMin) degree from Fuller Theological Seminary. Walt has served churches for thirty-seven years in a pastoral role. Walt has served his local ICF Colorado chapter as a board member and as credentialing director. He also was director of credentialing for Christian Coaches Network, International (CCNI). Walt has served coaching schools as an instructor and mentor coach. Walt and his wife, Sharon, live in Golden, Colorado, where they are active in their local church. They enjoy skiing, hiking, and traveling.

www.ingramcontent.com/pod-product-compliance
Lightning Source LLC
Chambersburg PA
CBHW021923190326

41519CB00009B/887